Occupational Health Psychology:
The Challenge of Workplace Stress

Occupational Health Psychology

The Challenge of Workplace Stress

Marc Schabracq, Cary Cooper,
Cheryl Travers and David van Maanen

THE BRITISH
PSYCHOLOGICAL
SOCIETY

First published in 2001 by BPS Books (The British Psychological Society),
St Andrews House, 48 Princess Road East, Leicester, LE1 7DR, UK.

A catalogue record for this book is available from the British Library.

ISBN 1 85433 327 5

Typeset by Book Production Services, London.
Printed in Great Britain by MPG Books Ltd.
Distributed by Plymbridge Distributors, Estover, Plymouth, PL6 7PZ, UK.

Contents

List of tables, figures and Self-Assesment Questionnaires   vii
About the authors   ix
Acknowledgements   xi

1. Introduction
  1.1 Background   1
  1.2 Stress as an indicator   1
  1.3 The objectives of our approach   2
  1.4 The undesired effects of stress   3
  1.5 Factors behind the increased interest in stress   7
  1.6 Outline of the book   8

2. What is stress?
  2.1 Everyday life   10
  2.2 Organizational culture   23
  2.3 Effective functioning of everyday working life   28
  2.4 Stress   38

3. Stress reactions and sources of stress
  3.1 Individual stress reactions   47
  3.2 Sources of stress   55

4. The approach
  4.1 Introduction   87
  4.2 Step 1: organization and consultant form a relationship   90
  4.3 Step 2: getting established   106
  4.4 Step 3: developing specific goals   113
  4.5 Step 4: designing interventions   120
  4.6 Step 5: reporting   124
  4.7 Step 6: implementation   131
  4.8 Step 7: evaluation   136

Addendum: Interventions
1 Introduction 139
2 Workshops 140
3 Coaching 148
4 Employee assistance programmes 150
5 Adjusting the work load 151
6 Job redesign 152
7 Interventions in careers 156
8 Education and training 160
9 Individual counselling 169
10 Stress consultants 170

References 171
Index 175

List of tables, figures and Self-Assessment Questionnaires

Self-Assessment Questionnaires

1.	Life Events Scale	17
2.	Daily Hassles Scale	19
3.	Changed Ways of Thinking Checklist	49
4.	Fight Elements Checklist	50
5.	Tension Checklist	51
6.	Loss of Pleasure and Motivation Checklist	52
7.	Bodily Complaints Checklist	53
8.	Illnesses Checklist	54
9.	Too Little Orderliness Checklist	57
10.	Too Much Orderliness Checklist	59
11.	Too Little Social Embedding Checklist	63
12.	Too Much Social Embedding Checklist	65
13.	Too Little Safety Checklist	68
14.	Too Much Safety Checklist	71
15.	Too Little Compatibility of Values and Goals Checklist	74
16.	Too Much Compatibility of Values and Goals Checklist	75
17.	Spillover Checklist	78
18.	Too Much Task Challenge Checklist	82
19.	Too Little Task Challenge Checklist	85

Tables

2.1.	Impossibilities, 'unthinkables', and 'unspeakables'	24
2.2.	Explanations, solutions and blind spots	25
2.3.	Values and convictions	34
2.4.	Possible goals or outcomes of work	36
4.1.	Checklist of outcomes of step 1	106

4.2. Researching organizational culture   111
4.3. Checklist of outcomes of step 2   113
4.4. Sick leave and other personnel data   117
4.5. Procedures for guaranteeing anonymity   118
4.6. Checklist of outcomes of step 3   119
4.7. Techniques for boosting creativity   121
4.8. Checklist of outcomes of step 4   124
4.9. Reporting of stress risks: contents   127
4.10. Checklist of outcomes of step 5   131
4.11. Checklist of outcomes of step 6   135
4.12. Checklist of outcomes of step 7   138

Figure

2.1. The stages of a stress process   41

About the authors

Marc J. Schabracq teaches courses on work and health psychology at the University of Amsterdam and is a consultant in human aspects of production and change to both profit and non-profit organizations. He is well-known as an author of 17 scholarly books and over 100 articles as well as media appearances and a novelist. Together with Cary Cooper and Jacques Winnubst, he is also editor of the internationally-known *Handbook of Work and Health Psychology*, published by John Wiley.

Cary C. Cooper is Professor of Organisational Psychology and Health at the Manchester School of Management (UMIST). He has authored over 80 books and 300 scholarly articles on different aspects of occupational health in general and stress in particular, and is a frequent contributor to the media. He is founding editor of the *Journal of Organizational Behaviour*, co-editor of *Stress Medicine* and the *International Journal of Management Review*. He is a Fellow of the BPS, the Royal Society of Arts, the Royal Society of Medicine and the Royal Society of Health. Currently, Professor Cooper is President of the British Academy of Management, a Companion of the Institute of Management and a Fellow of the American Academy of Management.

Cheryl Travers teaches in the Business School, Loughborough University, where she has held several posts the most recent being Director of Doctoral Training. Her research interests and publications are various: occupational stress; management of change; women in management; and the impact of personality type on adaptation to work. She acts as a Consultant in most areas of management development, in particular, stress management and the management of change, to clients in both the public and the private sectors. She is co-author, with Cary Cooper, of *Teachers Under Pressure: Stress in the Teaching Profession*, published by Routledge.

David J van Maanen is a psychologist and business administration consultant on the implementation of change in both profit and non-profit organizations. His work includes coaching managers and teams in goal-setting and realizing change. He also teaches the subject of organizational health to post-graduates in the Netherlands.

Acknowledgements

This book stems from a project, devised by the Dutch 'Ministry of Public Health, Well-being and Sports' and the Arbo Management Group (AMG), to create a so-called 'stress management toolkit'. 'The Challenge of Workplace Stress' presents an approach for dealing with stress-related complaints in order to create a more effective organization.

Special thanks go to Dr. C.S.H.H. Dresens, for contributions to the Dutch version of the text, Dr. L.Y. Zijderveld, whose original case formed the basis for the approach described in chapter 4, and finally I want to express my gratitude to Jenny Roberts for time spent editing the English text.

Marc Schabracq, December 2000
(schabracq@psy.uva.nl)

1. Introduction

1.1 BACKGROUND

The last few decades have witnessed enormous and rapidly moving economic and technological change. These changes have been boosted by escalating worldwide competition, for which the stakes are becoming increasingly high. In spite of the negative consequences of this process, there is no indication that any global de-escalation is imminent. 'Survival of the fittest' remains the guiding principle, but the adaptation required does not relate to more or less stable environmental demands. What counts now is the pace at which we, collectively as well as individually, can adapt to a rapidly changing environment, a kind of 'survival of the fitting' (Morgan, 1986). This relates to our ability to anticipate and to successfully adapt to each change as it arises, without experiencing unnecessary stress and disruption. The ability to change without stress has become crucial for further organizational and personal development, and is likely to become one of the most important strategic factors for global competitive advantage. This book is about developing this ability to adapt.

1.2 STRESS AS AN INDICATOR

Outlined in this book is an approach that not only enables you to prevent or counteract stress, but suggests ways in which the frequent occurrence of work stress and its effects can be used to develop more effective organizational and personal resources and skills. In effect, it takes the reader through various 'project' stages by presenting relevant information about, and illustrations of, the causes and effects of stress, and at the same time giving the reader a chance to pause and reflect on aspects of their own organization – hence building up a picture of stress in their own work environment with which to work out solutions.

We start with the following two premises:

- When an individual or an organization reacts to stress this affects their ability to adapt to their environment. As such, these reactions will result in a multitude of costly and undesirable consequences.
- The frequent occurrence of stress-related complaints in a particular work environment can be an important indication that adaptation to that environment is fraught with problems, and many other subsequent difficulties may also result.

Stress has come to be regarded as a modern manifestation of evil. However – though we certainly do not typify stress as desirable – it can have some uses too, in that it can be a valuable indicator of individual and organizational health and well-being. If a significant number of people in a particular workplace are experiencing stress, we can assume that something about the nature of the work itself or the actual work environment must be fundamentally inappropriate and over-demanding and stress may be only one of a whole host of undesirable symptoms. In this way, stress provides us with an opportunity to trace 'systemic errors' in the way the organization functions and make this open for discussion. This enables both individual employees and the organization as a whole to devise structural improvements that also imply a better adaptation to the outside world in general.

Point for Reflection
Within which departments or jobs do the most stress-related reactions manifest themselves in your organization? What underlying factors might play a part here? What 'systemic errors' are operating here? What can be done about these underlying factors?

1.3 THE OBJECTIVES OF OUR APPROACH

Beginning with the premise that frequently occurring stress-related outcomes can be an indicator of inadequate organizational functioning, our approach focuses on these dysfunctional aspects, both in the direct work environment and in the actual work itself. The rationale behind this is that work and the environment within which it takes place must be designed in such a way that employees can keep their attention on their work in a self-evident and satisfying way. So any stress project goes beyond just preventing and counteracting stress and focuses foremost on creating better ways to work and better work environments. In recognizing and acknowledging the need to reduce the potential risk from stress, the most important guidelines and challenges that you can offer your organization and its employees are that they should strive in their everyday work for greater levels of:

- creativity, as well as more personal and professional development;
- effectiveness and better production quality;
- work satisfaction and motivation.

Our key objective in counteracting stress is having, as a starting point, an image of the organization in which we would like to work and the way in which this differs from our organization in its present state. This way we can find out what we should change and how we might bring these changes about. The purpose then of our approach is to enable an organization to cope with its stress problems by improving the way it functions, and to anchor this approach in its organizational culture as a continuous process. This has to be a matter for each individual organization, and should be – as much as possible – independent of external consultants. To realize this objective, a project team devised from members of the organization itself is put in place. We train this team to independently implement a stress management project and to anchor it in the organization. After the project's completion, the team members can go on serving as consultants for assessing the level of risk from stress and the likely outcomes and reactions.

The key first stage in this process is as follows: first, the project team studies the opportunities and limitations that the current organizational status quo offers. This involves examining aspects of organizational culture such as resistance to change, employees' own suggestions for improvement, other possible interventions and a thorough review of stress-related risks and reactions, sick leave, and other relevant data which personnel can provide. In a series of workshops, the project team members, employees, and a departmental or team manager then map out the local sources of stress and their causes and what must be done to cope with these. It is important here to deal first with the most important sources of stress as well as with those that are deemed easiest to influence (the latter because of the importance of a 'quick success' to start with). Issues that the unit or department itself can deal with are then under the discretion of those who are directly involved and they need to reach agreements on suitable interventions and, following discussion with the team members, subsequent appropriate action. They can, in principle, dispose of the whole current human resources set of interventions, and instead suggest other ways of organizing the work, other ways of managing, job redesign, career interventions, education, coaching and training programmes, among others in the area of stress management and, in addition, other specific interpersonal skills training. It is the purpose of this book to allow the reader to 'look over the shoulder' of other professionals in designing and carrying out such a project.

Point for Reflection
Think back to the solutions you offered in the previous Point for Reflection and, taking into account what has been said in this section of the book, how could you make your solutions: more effective and efficient; more instructive and development-oriented; more satisfying and motivating?

1.4 THE UNDESIRED EFFECTS OF STRESS

The fact that frequently occurring stress-related symptoms are an indicator of underlying systemic errors in the day-to-day functioning of an organization is not the only reason for seeking ways to improve the situation. Another important point is that stress is also a very unpleasant phenomenon in itself, with very unpleasant consequences, both for individual employees and organizations as a whole. Attempts to counteract and prevent the effects of stress are in the interests of all involved parties, which is another good reason to use it as an opportunity for Organization Development.

For an individual employee, the negative consequences of stress may consist of:

- loss of creativity and stagnation of personal development;
- loss of work motivation and pleasure;
- diminished effectiveness;
- a decrease of quality of life and work, and of personal well-being

- various psychological and physical complaints that can contribute to premature death.

We want to emphasize here that stress is not to be confused with hard work, tension, effort and high levels of activity. Each of these can enable us to turn in a top-class performance and the 'positive pressure' from these can all be part of a challenging life. Stress is different because of the lack or loss of control. So 'positive stress' does not exist: stress is by definition an unpleasant state, and insufficient control over our own actions is its main cause.

Point for Reflection
To what degree do you recognize the negative consequences of stress in other people within your organization?

To what degree do you recognize the negative consequences of stress in yourself?

For organizations, stress can lead to outcomes that can jeopardize their position in the marketplace. Some of the key effects are:

- low production quality and quantity;
- conflicts, ineffective co-operation, and disturbed relationships;
- failing communication with, and loss of, clients and suppliers;
- high turnover of well-qualified employees who are hard to replace;
- damage to the corporate image and negative public relations, making it hard to find new employees;
- high costs of sick leave and work disability, as well as of hiring and training temporary replacements.

Sick leave expenses are often the most noticeable effect, and these costs often present the most important impetus for tackling stress management. The primary reason is that sick leave is relatively easy to quantify and measure (if we restrict ourselves to calculating only the extra costs of replacement). Organizations often hold their line managers responsible for sick leave taken in their department. Though sick leave in itself is a completely legitimate immediate cause for a stress management project, there is a risk that a one-sided emphasis on sick leave can conceal other, often much bigger, costs. Another effect of such a one-sided approach is that many organizations confine themselves to better monitoring and guidance of sick leave and reintegration of long-term sick employees. In this way, they ignore the underlying causes of stress phenomena, and overlook the negative way in which they persistently influence the organization.

This brings us to the important point that you, as an instigator/ consultant of a stress management project within your organization, should incorporate the hidden costs of the effect of stress in your proposal. This does not mean that you have to offer in advance a precise estimation of the project's expenses and beneficial outcomes, which would be impossible. However, it does mean that you should point out these stress-related costs plus a review of actual costs if there is to be no stress management intervention. This, together with a general indication of the project's potential contributions to improvement in these areas, can be an appropriate lever to get the project under way.

In general, it is not the absolute outcome of the project that matters here, but the comparative advantage that such a project can offer. An improvement does not need to be complete or even very substantial in order to provide the organization with a better competitive position against other organizations. Indeed even a small improvement may make the difference between survival and failure. Box 1.1 provides an excellent illustration of this idea of comparative advantage.

Box 1.1 Comparative advantage

Two tourists go on a lion hunt together. They have provided themselves with the complete gear, including heavy rifles and sturdy hunting boots. The hunt is carried out in an elated atmosphere. No lion appears, but they shoot away all their ammunition at everything that moves. Walking back to their hotel, they suddenly encounter an enormous lion. The tourists look at each other. Then one of them sits down on a rock and starts taking off his boots.

"Why are you taking your boots off?" asks the other.

"Without boots, I can run faster."

"So you think that you can run faster than a lion?"

"No, of course not, but then again, I can run faster than you now."

Point for Reflection
What undesired consequences does stress have in your organization? Make estimations of the expenses attached to each consequence.

How are your competitors doing in this respect? What does that imply to you?

If there are considerable differences, how could these be accounted for? What could you learn from them in this respect?

1.5 FACTORS BEHIND THE INCREASED INTEREST IN STRESS

It goes without saying that stress is an issue of contemporary importance. The media, for example, mention it almost on a daily basis. Apart from the many undesired effects of stress, other factors play a role here too, including the following:

• increases in certain factors causing stress, such as change, the shift from physical to mental work tasks, scarcity of well-educated employees in certain sectors, and so on (see sections 2.3 and 3.2);
• the ageing working population and their attitudes to change;
• growing insight into the nature of stress as a process and the speed at which it can spread;
• social legislation and claims for compensation for stress-related complaints;
• the increased popularity of human resource management (HRM)

On the last point, HRM considers a company's employees to be a form of organizational capital. Exposing employees to stress unnecessarily, then, becomes a foolish way of de-investing and destroying one's capital. A similar argument applies when we depart from the concept of 'employability', that is, an individual remaining employable in a way that sufficiently contributes to our own effectiveness, motivation, and development options. Here, however, the responsibility lies more with the individual employee than with the organization.

Point for Reflection
Has your organization been involved in a merger during the last ten years? What were the consequences in terms of stress? How did the organization take care of these consequences? What still remains to be done?

What other changes affected the organization and its employees? Did stress effects occur? How were these dealt with?

How about personnel shortages and temporary or permanent work overload? What can and should you do about it?

What does your employees' age distribution look like? Do the different age groups get sufficient attention when it comes to training or specific age-related problems?

1.6 OUTLINE OF THE BOOK

This book offers information about stress, an approach to stress management, and a review of further interventions. It is intended as a textbook for HR professionals, consultants, project leaders, and other team members who lead and implement stress management projects that focus on changing organizational processes. These may be employees from the organization itself as well as external consultants.

Chapters 2 and 3 discuss what we mean by stress, what causes it, and how we can recognize it. These chapters offer a solid background for carrying out a stress management project and its associated interventions, and use insights from different theories and research areas to arrive at a new, coherent description of the whole process.

In chapter 2, we set stress alongside normal functioning in everyday work reality, elucidate the role of organizational culture, and look at the mechanics of the stress process. Stress occurs when we have to keep our attention on our work, while unable or unwilling to do so due to aspects of our work, the working environment, and ourselves. The perceived and actual lack of control resulting from this can evoke a stress reaction.

In chapter 3, the different stress-related reactions and sources are reviewed extensively. The central theme within this section is that too much or too little of certain characteristics in our work and its environment are often the greatest source of stress.

Chapter 4 provides an overview of our approach to stress management. Educating and working with a project team so that it has a thorough knowledge of this approach is essential to the success of the project. In this chapter we outline the various stages and aspects such as the preparation of the project, the parties and disciplines involved, implementing a stress management project structure, and communicating about the project. The design and application of research into the causes and effects of stress is also dealt with, and we outline suggested research questions, instruments, and procedures. In addition, we discuss some of the more political aspects of such a project, e.g. conflicts of interest, resistance, and employees' suggestions for improvement. A project leader must be able to handle and make use of resistance. Having an insight into change processes is also very important when it comes to managing such a project, as is insight into organizational culture – the normal ways of acting, thinking, and feeling in the organization with its specific 'unspeakables'. The way in which an organization takes decisions; recognizes, discusses, and solves work problems; the pace with which employees usually implement changes; all these are factors that can influence a successful implementation of a stress management project. This requires some 'historical' research into the background of the organization, which demands great openness, trust and courage from all parties involved. In the rest of chapter 4, we discuss goal setting for projects, and planning and implementing an intervention. Finally, we consider the project's evaluation and the options stemming from it, such as possibilities for improving the approach, anchoring it in the organization, and maintaining it.

An extended addendum reviews the broad range of specific interventions for stress management. Knowledge about possible interventions is indispensable to all those involved in the project implementation. Suggested interventions focus on the different levels of an organization: i.e. the organization as a whole, by department, group, specific jobs or functions, and individuals themselves. Most interventions stem from general HRM practice and only a small number are designed specifically for stress management.

2. What is stress?

What is stress? And what does stress at work mean? These questions are not as simple as they sound. That is why it is necessary to step aside and ask ourselves a few other questions first. What does a life without stress look like? How does it relate to the world of work and to our organizational culture? When these questions are answered satisfactorily, it will be much simpler to answer our original questions concerning the nature of stress. In this chapter, we deal with the following issues and how they link to stress:

- everyday life;
- organizational culture: the everyday environment of work;
- effective functioning of everyday working life;
- stress.

2.1 EVERYDAY LIFE

Before we examine stress in the workplace, we need to consider our lives outside work and certain related psychological and behavioural processes that help build up a picture of how we come to experience stress.

Repetition

What is the most striking feature of our everyday life? The most obvious answer is that there is no very striking feature; it is all so familiar. Nothing much occurs unexpectedly. In our everyday life, we do not go through many new experiences: most things happen, more or less, in ways that we are used to. Everyday life is a matter of repetition.

One thing that *is* characteristic of our daily life is our striving toward stability and repetition. We choose attractive surroundings and subject them, as much as possible, to our tastes and preferences. In this way, we shape our environment. The next step consists of adapting ourselves to this self-designed environment. We develop fixed rules of conduct and fixed ways of dividing our attention, to which we cling and which we repeat with a kind of calm fanaticism. In this way, we become specialized: we develop our own reality, a relatively stable niche to live and work in (see Schabracq, 1991).

This applies to our whole life. For example, most of us live in one house, with a small number of other people, and have our unchangeable daily, weekly, and yearly routines. This also applies to our work. Most of us work at a well-known site, at more or less fixed hours of the day, following well-known routines. We do so alone or with a limited number of acquaintances, with whom we relate in fixed ways. When it comes to coffee, lunch, and tea breaks, we also tend to have our predictable habits and preferences. Though there are considerable differences between people in this respect, the variety in our daily life at work is essentially very limited, at least compared to the endless possibilities that reality has to offer.

To elaborate a little more, imagine a normal working day. We rise each day at the same time with the help of an alarm clock. Then we follow the utterly familiar routines of going to the toilet, washing, and dressing. We shave or put on our makeup in our usual way. In the background, the radio or television provides familiar programmes with familiar people, who talk about familiar subjects. We eat our usual breakfast. If we work away from home, we go to work 'on time' and by a familiar route. Generally, the work also occurs in a fixed, familiar environment. Here, we do our usual work, in the company of familiar people, who are present every day. At more or less fixed hours we pause, have a chat, drink some coffee, and eat our preferred lunch. When it is 'time', we go home, again by a fixed route, where we eat dinner, again according to our usual preference. Then we dedicate ourselves to filling our leisure time in our usual ways. Finally we undress, wash, clean our teeth, and go to bed. There, we may indulge in some sexual activity, but then, after having set our alarm clock, we are overtaken by sleep and lose consciousness again.

So it goes on, for most people, for five days a week. At the weekend, things are different, though still very predictable. During the holidays, things are even more different, but here also we go out of our way to establish fixed routines. In short, when we look without prejudice at a usual working day, we can only be surprised at the immense quantity of repetition it involves. For example, think of all those familiar thoughts, feelings, smells, and other sensations that we evoke on a single day by our normal ways of acting and our everyday conversations. Are these not precisely the experiences that tell us that we are our normal selves? We are constantly busy rebuilding and re-enacting our surrounding reality. Being ourselves obviously takes a lot of work.

Point for Reflection
Having read the description of a working day, sit back, relax, and try to recollect a typical workday of your own. What are its typical elements? How does it start?

How do your preferences steer you through a typical day? What routines make up your work and leisure time?

What does this way of living do for you?

Discipline of attention as a way of coping

A key thing about our everyday lives is that we could not possibly attend to everything that goes on around us and so we tend to be selective. This is all a matter of self-discipline: we attend only to what matters to us and concerns us, and ignore the rest. We just don't pay attention to most of what – and who – can be seen or experienced at work. In the elevator or in the canteen, for example, we hardly pay attention to employees whom we don't know personally, even when their faces look familiar. These kinds of situations, where we find ourselves in the presence of people with whom we don't interact, demonstrate our perceptual discipline.

By keeping to the 'rules of irrelevance' (Goffman, 1972), we prevent ourselves from being needlessly lost in contacts with accidental passers-by. We do this in an almost ritual way by showing 'civil inattention'. Our gaze passes quickly over the other person as a sign that we are aware of his or her presence and that we do not mind this. Then we look away without any sign of recognition, to show that we don't want further contact. It is a form of politeness, by which we show to others that, though we consider them to be a 'complete' person, we do not have any special interest in them and do not have any special intention towards them (Goffman, 1963, p.84). Paying civil inattention is normal conduct in such a situation, and most of the time we don't notice it. These however only really become obvious to us when other people or we ourselves violate these rules. This occurs when a stranger stares at us or when a stranger catches us studying him or her secretly. In both cases, this can evoke in us unpleasant feelings of alarm and uneasiness (Schabracq, 1991, pp.140–1).

This way of paying attention selectively enables us to stay in the situation at hand as if it were the only possible reality at that moment. When we are in these certain circumstances, we actively shield ourselves from all others that are possible. We do so by not paying any special attention to these other situations, and by clearly showing that this is what we are doing. Thus we actively prevent ourselves from being involved in unexpected events and, even if we fail to prevent this happening, we still have our own ways of not becoming completely distracted and absorbed by them.

In this way, the reality of everyday life shows clear 'borders', over which we rarely pass. We do not experience these as actual borders, though, because we do not pay attention to them. They are the result of habit, our usual ways of acting and perceiving. Usually however, we share these particular ways of acting and perceiving with other people in our environment, who live and work in the same way as we do. In other words, this way of dividing our attention is culturally determined (see section 2.2 below). This makes it incomprehensible to people who are not thoroughly introduced to our culture in everyday life (e.g. strangers, small children) or organizational life (e.g. new employees, suppliers, customers)

Examples of how we limit our reality to what we pay attention to are described in the following extracts:

> *There are no annoying 'gaps' in the reality of things. Attention is not focused on places where there is nothing to attend to. It is as if one moves through a landscape of stage wings, designed by a competent magician, who takes care that our attention is divided each time we approach a situational border.*
>
> (Schabracq, 1987, p.127)

> *The apparent continuity of consciousness that exists in everyday normal awareness is in fact a precarious illusion that is only made pos-*

sible by the associative connections between related bits of conversa-
tion, task orientation and so on. We have all experienced the instant
amnesia that occurs when we go too far on some tangent so we 'lose
the thread of thought' or 'forget just what we were going to do'.
Without the bridging associative connections, consciousness would
break down into a series of discrete states with as little continuity as is
apparent in our dream life

(Erickson, Rossi & Rossi, 1976, p.299)

I imagine, sometimes, that if a film could be made of one's life, every
other frame would be death. It goes so fast we're not aware of it.
Destruction and resurrection in alternate beats of being, but speed
makes it seem continuous. But you see, kid, with ordinary conscious-
ness you can't even begin to know what's happening.

(Bellow, 1982, p.295)

This way of limiting our everyday reality enables us to stay in the
familiar situations that are conducive to reaching our goals. In other
words, it keeps our attention free for our work and other issues
which we see as important, and can greatly improve the quality of
that work. It is a common, culturally determined form of coping, a
way of acting that makes it possible to attain our goals while preventing us from experiencing stress.

Point for Reflection
During the next few days, make a point of observing the 'borders' of your
own attention and those of other bystanders and passers-by. Good places to
practise are canteens, bars, shops, elevators, public transport, and waiting
rooms: places where you are in the presence of others with whom you don't
have any further communication.

Where do you look? Where do they look? How do you hold your body, and
how do they hold theirs? What happens when you look people in the eye?
How does that feel?

Denial

Besides 'borders', reality can also show 'holes'. In order to prevent
disturbance of our performance, we sometimes don't pay attention to
issues that other people notice immediately. In such a case, we speak
of 'denial', a way of subduing experiences or suppressing them completely, which we can apply in a well-directed and measured way.

Just as in the case of situational borders, we do this because it is the only way to keep our attention on our immediate goals. In the stress literature, denial is presented as an instance of passive coping. The more drastic forms of denial – the big holes – demand that we fill the resulting emptiness with something that is less threatening, disturbing, or disagreeable (Dorpat, 1985). Sometimes this means that we focus on something else, something that offers stimuli that are likely to hold our attention. At other times, it means that we tacitly 'fill' the resulting hole with the same material of which the borders and the wider environment of the hole are made.

Breznitz (1983) distinguishes seven forms of cognitive denial:

- denial of relevance to one's own person ('It doesn't matter to me');
- denial of urgency ('We don't have to deal with that now');
- denial of the relevance to our own vulnerability or responsibility ('It doesn't hurt me', or 'That isn't my department');
- denial of a feeling about something ('I don't feel a thing');
- denial of the relevance of a feeling ('I'm not angry because of that – I just got out of the bed on the wrong side');
- denial of the threatening character of information ('Whatever it is, it's not serious');
- denial of all relevant information ('There's nothing going on', or 'There's nothing wrong').

In addition, there are other forms of denial involving perception. These may vary from overlooking something or someone, to so-called negative hallucinations (the disappearance of a certain object from the perceptive field) and the total breakdown of a complete sensory system, in the case of hysterical blindness and deafness – all phenomena that can be produced by hypnosis. Bandler and Grinder (1986) describe, for example, a hypnosis session, during which the well-known hypnotherapist Erickson contrived for body-parts of the writer Aldous Huxley to 'disappear', to the great surprise of the latter.

Point for Reflection

For a few days, make a point of observing your own reactions while reading the papers or looking at the television news. Do certain news item evoke emotions such as sorrow, disgust, hate, shame and anxiety in you? Do you feel these emotions fully?

Which of the seven above-mentioned forms of denial are your favourites? To what degree do you differ on this point from your friends and family? What impact does this use of denial have on you and how you cope with everyday life and events?

Interference

We all have our fixed approaches to the people and events that, notwithstanding the discipline of our attention, still penetrate the borders of our everyday reality. A useful way of understanding how this takes place is Lazarus's theory of primary and secondary appraisal (Lazarus, 1966) First, a quick assessment of what is going on takes place. Lazarus's 'primary appraisal' asks: is this a threat? And then: is this important, pleasant, annoying, urgent, or whatever? Lazarus's 'secondary appraisal' follows: do we have to do something about this; what can we do; what routine is applicable here ('active coping')? Or: is it better to ignore it ('passive coping')? To do so, we usually choose instantly from our repertoire of fixed coping responses. Only rarely do we invent something new, in order to store it with some pleasure – at least, if it is successful – in our repertoire of coping responses.

Neither form of appraisal costs us much attention or effort. Because we ourselves have designed our environment and we know it so well, we know exactly what to attend to. So an almost automatic check suffices to establish whether something is going on which demands our further attention (Lindsey & Norman, 1977). When an event interferes with our work or threatens us, in such a way that we cannot counteract it effectively, this can give rise to stress (see section 2.4 below). Such an occurrence can be a 'life event', that demands a fundamental adaptation of our everyday life, the niche in which we live. However, it can also be a 'daily hassle', an unavoidable nuisance which, however, does not demand an essential adaptation.

Life events

Far-reaching events in our life – so-called life events – are those that demand an essential reorganization of our life. These can be events that were to be expected, inasmuch as they happen to most people and are part of normal personal development with its varying life stages, transitions, and crises, such as marriage, moving house, and changing jobs. Then there are events that occur more unexpectedly, even if their occurrence is statistically quite likely. Examples here are the death of a loved one, accidents, or a divorce. The common denominator to all these events is that they temporarily unsettle our lives. Certain aspects of our lives or key people are no longer there or have suddenly become unimportant. What is now important is not yet clear. Our fixed ways of dividing our attention and fixed lines of conduct no longer make sense. All this can also apply to positive life events such as a big personal success or winning a large amount in a lottery.

In each case, successful adaptation requires the taking our leave of the state existing before the event, working through the emotions accompanying it, recovering ourselves at a new point of departure, and developing new ways of thinking, acting, and feeling. Problems arise when we cling to the previous situation and arrive at an impasse. When this carries on for too long, we risk ending up in a serious depressive state.

Holmes and Rahe (1967) declared that the occurrence of many life events during the previous years was supposed to increase the chance of a life-threatening disease considerably. Though empirical studies do not provide corroboration for this, life events may still lead to serious stress reactions. The Life Events Scale measures the occurrence and impact of such events in your own life. A remarkable feature of these items is that they cover the same subjects that fill our TV programmes and popular magazines.

Self-Assessment Questionnaire – 1

Life Events Scale

Place a cross (X) in the 'Yes' column for each event that has taken place in the last two years. Then circle a number on the scale that best describes how upsetting the event was to you, e.g. a 10 for death of spouse.

Event	Yes	Scale
Bought house	___	1 2 3 4 5 6 7 8 9 10
Sold house	___	1 2 3 4 5 6 7 8 9 10
Moved house	___	1 2 3 4 5 6 7 8 9 10
Major house renovation	___	1 2 3 4 5 6 7 8 9 10
Separation of loved one	___	1 2 3 4 5 6 7 8 9 10
End of relationship	___	1 2 3 4 5 6 7 8 9 10
Got engaged	___	1 2 3 4 5 6 7 8 9 10
Got married	___	1 2 3 4 5 6 7 8 9 10
Marital problem	___	1 2 3 4 5 6 7 8 9 10

Awaiting divorce	___	1 2 3 4 5 6 7 8 9 10
Divorce	___	1 2 3 4 5 6 7 8 9 10
Child started nursery/school	___	1 2 3 4 5 6 7 8 9 10
Increased nursing responsibilities		
for elderly or sick person	___	1 2 3 4 5 6 7 8 9 10
Problems with relatives	___	1 2 3 4 5 6 7 8 9 10
Problems with friends/neighbours	___	1 2 3 4 5 6 7 8 9 10
Pet-related problems	___	1 2 3 4 5 6 7 8 9 10
Work-related problems	___	1 2 3 4 5 6 7 8 9 10
Change in nature of work	___	1 2 3 4 5 6 7 8 9 10
Threat of redundancy	___	1 2 3 4 5 6 7 8 9 10
Changed job	___	1 2 3 4 5 6 7 8 9 10
Made redundant	___	1 2 3 4 5 6 7 8 9 10
Unemployed	___	1 2 3 4 5 6 7 8 9 10
Retired	___	1 2 3 4 5 6 7 8 9 10
Increased or new bank loan/		
mortgage	___	1 2 3 4 5 6 7 8 9 10
Financial difficulty	___	1 2 3 4 5 6 7 8 9 10
Insurance problem	___	1 2 3 4 5 6 7 8 9 10
Legal problem	___	1 2 3 4 5 6 7 8 9 10
Emotional or physical illness of		
close family or relative	___	1 2 3 4 5 6 7 8 9 10
Serious illness of close family or		
relative requiring hospitalization	___	1 2 3 4 5 6 7 8 9 10
Surgical operation experienced by		
family member or relative	___	1 2 3 4 5 6 7 8 9 10
Death of spouse	___	1 2 3 4 5 6 7 8 9 10
Death of family member or relative	___	1 2 3 4 5 6 7 8 9 10
Death of close friend	___	1 2 3 4 5 6 7 8 9 10
Emotional or physical illness		
of yourself	___	1 2 3 4 5 6 7 8 9 10
Serious illness or accident requiring		
your own hospitalization	___	1 2 3 4 5 6 7 8 9 10
Surgical operation on yourself	___	1 2 3 4 5 6 7 8 9 10
Pregnancy	___	1 2 3 4 5 6 7 8 9 10
Birth of baby	___	1 2 3 4 5 6 7 8 9 10
Birth of grandchild	___	1 2 3 4 5 6 7 8 9 10
Family member left home	___	1 2 3 4 5 6 7 8 9 10
Difficult relationship with children	___	1 2 3 4 5 6 7 8 9 10
Difficult relationship with parents	___	1 2 3 4 5 6 7 8 9 10

Use the following rough guide as an indicator of the potential stress level caused by your recent life events.

Low stress		High stress
1	50	100

Adapted from Cooper and Cartwright (1997)

Daily hassles

Daily hassles (Kanner et al., 1981) are small but irritating events that interfere with our daily routines, as well as with the image of ourselves that we want to project, but do not demand a reorganization of our life. We just try to counteract their effects, or pay them as little attention as possible. Think of the following succession of events, the harvest of a bad day. Our alarm clock does not go off. Our car refuses to start or the bus is late. A cup of coffee spills over our new suit. Some colleagues fail to keep their appointment and cannot make another time for us. As stress sources, the effects of daily hassles add up. Though a great number of these events can affect our immune system (Brosschot, 1991), it is unlikely that anyone with a healthy heart will die of them. As it is, we are not helplessly at the mercy of these events: the design of everyday life, as outlined previously in this section, aims to prevent such events or minimize their effects.

There is a 'chicken-and-egg' problem here: do we suffer from stress by daily hassles or are we more prone to running into these because we are already suffering from stress and are not observing our routines closely enough? Or does our being stressed mean that we are more likely to experience or perceive events as hassles?

Self-Assessment Questionnaire – 2

Daily Hassles Scale: How was your day?

At the end of the day, place a cross (X) in the 'Yes' column for each event that has taken place during this day. Then circle a number on the scale that best describes how upsetting the event crossed was to you.

Event	Yes	No stress at all		Stress		A great deal of stress	
Stumbling	___	0	1	2	3	4	5
Being late	___	0	1	2	3	4	5
Being pestered	___	0	1	2	3	4	5
Oversleeping	___	0	1	2	3	4	5
Missing your bus/train	___	0	1	2	3	4	5
Car trouble	___	0	1	2	3	4	5
Other transport trouble	___	0	1	2	3	4	5

A small accident	__	0	1	2	3	4	5
Getting your clothes dirty	__	0	1	2	3	4	5
Being ridiculed	__	0	1	2	3	4	5
Stepping into something dirty	__	0	1	2	3	4	5
Annoying insects	__	0	1	2	3	4	5
Bothersome noise	__	0	1	2	3	4	5
Unpleasant smell	__	0	1	2	3	4	5
Dirty furniture	__	0	1	2	3	4	5
Constant interruptions	__	0	1	2	3	4	5
Being unable to find something	__	0	1	2	3	4	5
Accidentally breaking something	__	0	1	2	3	4	5
Appointments that are not met	__	0	1	2	3	4	5
Spilling your drink	__	0	1	2	3	4	5
Forgetting to do something	__	0	1	2	3	4	5
Making mistakes	__	0	1	2	3	4	5
Being harassed	__	0	1	2	3	4	5
Getting lost	__	0	1	2	3	4	5
Bumping yourself	__	0	1	2	3	4	5
Being treated rudely	__	0	1	2	3	4	5
Being accused of something	__	0	1	2	3	4	5
Promises that are not kept	__	0	1	2	3	4	5

Use the following rough guide as an indicator of the potential level of stress caused by the number of daily hassles that you experience.

Low stress	High stress
0-10	>25

Systemic factors behind life events and daily hassles

An interesting point – and a central one in this book – is that, although the occurrence of life events and daily hassles can appear to be purely coincidental, they can often be traced to specific factors, especially when they occur with great frequency. Some people, for example, attract such events. We can usually find simple reasons for this, such as habitually paying too little attention to one's environment, health problems, procrastination, taking on too much work, or not being able or willing to manage one's affairs properly. Some organizations too are so chaotic that fighting everyday hassles appears to be their main business, and they don't allow themselves the necessary time and effort to deal with the underlying causes. In addition, some of these disturbances may be a result of unwilling-ness – both at the individual and organizational level – to face the fact that serious changes have taken place that demand a radical reorientation and adaptation.

As suggested previously in Chapter 1, the frequent occurrence of stress-related complaints can be a sign of an underlying system error, which has far-reaching consequences. To put it bluntly: people are unwillingly and unknowingly serving as 'mine canaries'. (These canaries were taken down mines to detect explosive gases, their detection work consisting of falling off their perches when overcome by too high a concentration of gas down the mine.)

Point for Reflection
Can you think of an example of an underlying factor in your organization that is the root cause of several kinds of stress complaints? Who are the mine canaries in your organization?

Outcomes

Though there are unlimited possibilities in our lives, we have disci-plined ourselves to constantly re-enact a repetitive life in a small niche, as though we have settled for operating a treadmill of our own making with which we keep our life familiar and predictable. What does such a life have to offer us?

The most important gain is that a certain degree of repetition enables us to develop skills, with the help of which we can even-tually deal with recurring situations automatically. This enables us to keep our attention on what is really important to us, for exam-ple, setting goals, taking on rewarding enterprises, or solving complex problems. Repetition thus results in a conveniently orga-nized life, which we experience as our own and as safe. Such a way of working enables us to develop sufficient grip on our work in order to: do our work effectively and efficiently; have pleasure in our work; and create sufficient possibilities for self-develop-ment.

This involves achieving a good fit between ourselves as individ-uals and the niches that we have chosen and designed for ourselves, through constantly re-enacting the routines attached to these niches. Ideally, this results in a good fit between what we want and are able to do, within the restrictions of what we are allowed and have to do. This provides a sound point of departure for effective, motivating and instructive activities. Coping then becomes the developing, maintaining, and repairing of such a fit.

The concept of a niche reminds us of what in ethology is known as a territory (Emlen, 1958; Kaufman, 1971): a space that an animal protects and defends. Intrusions on, or loss of, a territory can give rise to violent emotions (Rowell, 1972) and stress-related responses (see section 2.4) which can sometimes lead to the death of the animal. Though there are important differences between animal and human territories, intrusions and partial loss give rise to comparable stress reactions in humans (Eibl-Eibesfeldt, 1970). Humans too cling to their routines, claims, and rights, and defend these if necessary.

Work as an independent domain of life

Ideally, our work offers us an independent domain of life in whose reality we can have faith (James, 1890/1950) and in which we can lose ourselves, in order to realize our personal goals and motives. Therefore work becomes an arena in which we can distinguish ourselves, win, and excel. People's preferences in this respect vary considerably, as shown by the following examples of work outcomes:

- Losing oneself completely in a difficult and demanding task in order to attain optimal performance. This can result in a kind of high that is known as 'flow' or 'optimal experience' (Csikszentmihalyi, 1990), as well as a valuable product or performance, and outcomes such as admiration and prestige.
- Losing ourselves in familiar tasks in order to reach a state of mental calm and cheerfulness. Our work then becomes the exercise of a ritual, a way of working that was once part of monastic life (the *vita meditans*; Arendt, 1958) and was recently preached by the Baghwan sect. Cleaning is a task especially suited for this purpose.
- Experiencing a great deal of social contact with colleagues, seen as the most important outcome of the kinds of simple work that provide ample opportunity for it.
- Working too much and too hard, in order to show what we can endure and to claim unconditional care and love at home. Though this can be easily diagnosed as masochism, it is practised frequently and enthusiastically (see also section 2.4).

Point for Reflection
To what degree do you recognize these forms of working from your own experience? What do they do for you?

2.2 ORGANIZATIONAL CULTURE

Of great influence on ourselves, and the way in which we experience work, is the culture of the organization in which we work. It is important to consider culture, especially as this will have a great impact on whether or not a stress management project can be successfully implemented.

What is organizational culture?

Normal working is closely related to what is considered normal in the environment in which we work. What do other people (colleagues, managers, and our staff) find normal and abnormal? And does that coincide with what we ourselves experience? What passes as normal and abnormal in an organization is a matter of the culture of that organization. The organizational culture determines what we do in that organization, but also how we do it, what we say about it, and even what we think and feel about it. The culture determines to a certain degree what is possible or impossible, thinkable or unthinkable, speakable or unspeakable within the organization (see Table 2.1). In this way, it determines what we are allowed and have to do, as well as what we are not allowed to do.

Point for Reflection
What are the important impossibilities, unthinkables, and unspeakables in your own organization? What are their effects?

Culture is the result of – as well as the pattern for – the ways in which the members of an organization usually solve their recurring everyday problems. As discussed in section 2.1, we can conceive organizational culture as an organization-specific form of coping: the successful adaptations that have resulted in the structure of the organization. So organizational culture refers to the structure, design, and rationale of organizational reality, in a material sense (buildings, machinery, furniture, symbols, clothes, behaviour, etc.) as well as in a non-material sense (values, convictions, norms, stories, atmosphere, typical approaches, attitudes, etc.).

Table 2.1: Impossibilities, 'unthinkables', and 'unspeakables'

Impossibilities are certain solutions, approaches, and policies, which cannot be applied or followed in a certain organization, because of the way the organization is currently structured. For example, in many organizations it is impossible to start up an organization-wide approach to stress management, just because of the taboo on talking about stress.

Unthinkables are certain solutions, approaches, and policies that cannot be put into words in an organization because they do not fit into the current organizational frame of reference. An example is the suggestion of giving permanent appointments at every British university to occupational shamans (e.g. occupational psychologists, occupational chaplains and welfare officers); or faith healers to deal with the personnel's stress problems.

Unspeakables are certain complaints, solutions, approaches, and policies that are articulated to reliable colleagues, but not to those who can make a difference on this issue. For example, employees complain among themselves that their manager is one of the causes of their stress, while they do not share this with the manager in question or with his or her superiors.

Effective intervention with regard to impossibilities, unthinkables, and unspeakables always boils down to a form of organizational change.

As an organization's culture stems from a fixed approach to standard problems, it also has its own unproductive standard explanations and standard ways to tackle problems, as well as its own blind spots. There is much rhetorical abuse and misuse of terms such as 'normal', 'really', 'truly', 'actually', 'simply', 'only', 'always', 'all', 'never' and 'nothing': words that are used as if to explain the effects of a law of nature that is 'actually' too simple to need explanation. The blind spots show clear similarities with the forms of denial discussed in section 2.1. Applied to stress problems, this may lead to the kind of remarks shown in Table 2.2.

These 'holes in the everyday reality' are not necessarily a matter of subconscious denial. It can also be a matter of strategically installed 'borders': 'That's not my business'; 'For access to that, you have to be in our human resources department'; or 'Even if that were true, they certainly wouldn't inform me'. This, of course, depends on where employees or managers draw their occupational boundaries.

Given that an organization really wants to prevent stress-related complaints, the question arises as to why people make such remarks, especially in light of the fact that the frequent occurrence of

---

Table 2.2: Explanations, solutions, and blind spots

Explanations

You must have spoken to Johnson. He's always complaining.

The causes lie in their private lives.

We have to work with the locals here and they always have something to nag about.

It's simply a matter of their age.

Women are just oversensitive, and not as emotionally strong as men are.

That's just the culture here.

Solutions

Maybe we should install a working party first.

I'll give Peterson a call.

This needs a thorough study first; this one's no good.

Johnson just needs a holiday.

Just don't pay attention to it.

Blind spots

Stress isn't an issue at all here.

Let's be reasonable about this: everything's going just fine here.

Working never killed anybody yet.

It's only a fad. A few years ago stress just didn't exist.

At least in my department, everything's all right.

Nobody told me.

---

stress-related outcomes clearly signals that there is a serious system error at work. A simple answer is that it is obviously seen as more important to leave the organizational culture intact than to risk it by intervening in possible stress-related problems.

Point for Reflection

Having read the remarks about standard explanations, solutions, and blind spots, make a point of observing these phenomena during meetings in your own organization.

What is their effect?

Resistance to change

Why is it apparently more important to leave the organizational culture intact than to deal with individual misery and possible organizational malfunctioning? Answers to this question can be found if we address the following:

- what it costs and benefits us to become part of the organizational culture;
- the fact that this is a shared process and we can support each other in our resistance to change;
- the reactions of 'outsiders' and the escalation in commitment they can bring about.

A first point is that we have all invested in the development and acceptance of our organizational culture. It took us time and effort to do this and we're proud to have succeeded in it. Now we reap the harvest of it: we know exactly what's expected of us and what we have to do without having to pay attention to it. This leaves our attention free for what is important. The manifested culture and the suppositions underlying it have become a part of ourselves – a part of which we are largely unaware. That is why we experience changes in these suppositions, particularly when imposed on us from the outside, as intrusions upon our own conduct and personality, even when they result in improvements.

Such changes require us to abandon our familiar orientation towards part of our daily life. This evokes a painful emotional process, which we would prefer to prevent and avoid. Moreover, it is a process that we share with our colleagues, so it is only logical to support each other in our denial and our unproductive explanations and policies in order to prevent a threatening change: 'How can we be wrong, when we all see it the same way!' This can make resistance surprisingly effective and well co-ordinated. The outsider who acts as a protagonist of a change – for instance, the implementation of a stress management project – usually has little understanding of this. If the outsider is part of a team, such as the project team assigned to implement stress management, it is easy for the team to become convinced that all the employees have gone mad. There may be a ring of truth to this too, because these blind spots and standard explanations certainly don't impress outsiders with their realism.

In such a context, terms such as 'resistance' and 'resistance to change' are often used. These terms come from the realm of psychoanalysis and refer to obscure irrational forces in the individual. As such, they come in very handy as a way to label employees who fight changes as irrational beings, while sounding scientific. Though using these terms can reinforce outsiders' belief in their own mental health ('They're insane, we're not'), it does not contribute anything positive to the change process.

Clearly, declaring all employees insane does help to convince them that change would be the best solution for everyone. This is not about truth, but about what the employees want to accomplish, namely no change. Examining the content of their words – which, given their obvious unreasonableness, is very tempting – will quickly escalate into a real conflict between the two groups, with all the accompanying emotions, followed by the employees' refusal of all communication. As a result, the status quo will be reinforced and the organizational culture will have effectively fended off the threatened intrusion.

Point for Reflection
What instances of resistance to change in your organization come to mind? How did you respond? Do you know where your own resistance came from?

The above makes clear how effective organizational self-protection can be. It does not mean that any attempt at change from the outside *per se* is doomed to fail, but it does mean that successful intervention is very difficult. There are no standard recipes here. We recommend that employees themselves are encouraged to express what is going on and what their basic suppositions are, as well as what they could change in this respect. The methods for achieving this vary. One way of doing this is to hold a meeting to encourage employee openness and communication. A good start for such a session is to determine the goal of the meeting: 'What do we want to accomplish?' During the meeting, you can always go back to this point: 'Are we actually doing what we wanted to do?' And if not: 'How did this come about? What can be done about it?' Ask questions about the process, reflect, ask about specifics, probe for specific examples, let employees articulate their feelings. In short, conduct a sort of group counselling session: 'Where are we now?', 'How are things going?', 'Is this what we want to happen?', 'What are we doing at this moment?', 'What has still to be done?' In addition, the 'outsider' can comment on the process ('This strikes me as...', 'Hearing this, I get the impression that...'), and provide information and advice, preferably only if asked for. If the outsider feels up to it, and has a talent for it, they can sometimes intervene in a paradoxical way: 'Actually, I see what you are getting at. Stress isn't that important. Yes, of course, it can make you ill, but then again, nobody is irreplaceable'. Or even more rudely: 'Of course, people who suffer from stress aren't the pick of the bunch', and so on, hoping this will evoke some 'Yes, but...' responses. But again, there is no such thing as a standard recipe.

A last point is that different parties can have very real interests in keeping things the way they are. These interests should be expressed, if possible, to discover how the parties involved can compensate each other for their possible losses. In a brainstorming session, we may find out how to 'enlarge the cake', making it a 'win–win' situation for all parties, to which they can all commit themselves. However, such an outcome is not always possible, because interests linked with the change can't always be brought out in the open. Even then, it is recommended that you at least try to explicate the unspeakables.

2.3 EFFECTIVE FUNCTIONING OF EVERYDAY WORKING LIFE

Everyday working life, like every form of reality, depends on the attention we pay to it. When we attend to something else, either through our senses or just in our thoughts, we temporarily abandon the reality of our work: we occupy ourselves elsewhere, and our work stops determining our actions.

We can do our work best when we pay the necessary attention to it automatically, without having to force ourselves. This means that the work has to engage us by itself. It also implies that the environment should not provide too much in the way of diversion that will demand our attention unnecessarily. If these conditions are met, we call a working situation effective and efficient: the working situation allows us to do our work well. We experience this effective functioning as self-confidence, trust, and control. It enables us to experience performing our task as the only possible reality at that moment. William James (1890/1950) speaks in a comparable context about faith in the reality of what occupies us.

Whether the everyday reality of work is instrumental depends on three kinds of factors: the work itself, the work environment, and ourselves. Concerning ourselves, instrumentality involves what we have to do and are willing, able, and allowed to do. This can be largely determined by the work itself and the work environment. We have to realize, however, that in everyday practice individual differences play an important role: what is too much or too little for some people may be exactly right for others.

Effective functioning turns out to be a kind of 'middle region', which we can describe with the help of a number of variables. 'Too much' or 'too little' of a variable implies a lower level of efficiency of the work and the work situation. Taking the variable 'task difficulty', for example, we can't perform a task that is too difficult, but a task that is too easy also causes problems. However, the right degree of difficulty, the 'middle region' – which varies for each individual – will ensure effective functioning. We can consider this as an illustration of a very old and widespread ethical concept, namely 'the narrow path of virtue' or 'the golden mean', a central concept in the thinking of Aristotle and Christian philosophy, as well as in classical Chinese philosophy.

We look first at the work environment, an important part of organizational culture. If an organization offers a reality of effectiveness – an environment that enables us to do our work well automatically – it has to provide certain conditions, which are indispensable for every kind of reality. These are for the greater part derived from the work of Solomon Asch (1971). Asch, however, formulated these criteria for the reality of hypnotic trance, with the specific purpose of proving that such a trance is really a very common phenomenon. We will look at the following conditions: orderliness; social embedding; safety; compatibility of values and goals; work as an autonomous domain of life; suitable physical working conditions.

Orderliness

Effective work environments are characterized by orderliness and neatness. Examples are: normal everyday behaviour, which shows that there is nothing unusual happening; everything and everybody in the right place; no disturbing elements in the environment that demand unnecessary attention; tools and other equipment ready for use, well kept, tidy, and conveniently displayed.

Because no part of an orderly and tidy work environment demands our special attention other than to maintain it, such a form of orderliness enables us to focus on our real work. Moreover, it allows us to check our environment for intrusions and disturbances quickly and almost automatically, because these stand out against an orderly background, which we know thoroughly.

We accentuate this orderliness by different stylistic means. We might achieve this by grouping together objects, or by the use of forms such as arrows, dots, or pictograms, or by colour coding, and so on, in order to emphasize or clarify items that need special attention. There is often a specific company style or logo that affects the design of many objects, from the writing paper to the lettering in the corridors, the coffee cups and the napkins in the canteen. This attention to design also applies to people's behaviour and appearance. This involves particular styles of speech, body language, and personal appearance, which are accepted as normal in an organization. Though these are based on tacit rules and are seldom the object of deliberate attention, transgressions (wrong behaviour, wrong clothes, etc.) are usually immediately obvious.

By enacting this behaviour, we continually supply each other with the right cues and relational suggestions to allow each other, and ourselves, to act in an obvious and logical way (Schabracq, 1991). Such a stylized display of orderliness – Harré (1979) talks about 'social muzak' – suggests the existence of a well-considered plan that ensures that everything goes as it is meant to go, and surprises are out of the question. This provides us all with a pleasant feeling of control and safety. This point of view also explains why tidying and cleaning can have a pleasant centring and calming effect.

It is clear, however, that orderliness must not become a goal in itself, in the sense that pursuing immaculate orderliness interferes with doing our work. All in all, a correct degree of orderliness enables us to keep our attention on our work, without unnecessary distractions.

Point for Reflection
How orderly is your organization? How would you describe your company style? How would you describe typical behaviour in your organization? How does the orderliness in your organization make you feel?

To what extent are you orderly?

Social embedding

Working in an organization, we develop a social network. There are the people who hired us; there are colleagues, superiors, subordinates, clients, and other external contacts. We develop personal preferences, and some contacts develop into personal and friendly relationships. We find protectors, as well as favourite subordinates, colleagues, and outside contacts. So we develop a social network of trusted people, to whom relating is pleasurable and who make 'business as usual' feasible.

Stress researchers have studied the effects of social networks mainly under the heading of 'social support' and have convincingly documented its direct therapeutic effects in various studies (Winnubst & Schabracq, 1996). Because there is little agreement about the definition of social support, we use the more general term 'social embedding' or 'embedding in a social network'. A good network has to: be sufficiently extended; spread over different organizational levels and departments; consist mostly of the people we find trustworthy; contain personal contacts; be used, nurtured, and further developed actively and skilfully.

Being embedded in such a network can provide pleasant social contacts, which can result in emotional support and contribute to a general sense of belonging and security. As such, they can help to relieve tension. As well as surrendering to the different kind of reality that is defined by being together, this is also a matter of emotional contagion. This involves being 'infected' by the other's pleasant mood, a phenomenon that is usually cited in the case of unpleasant feelings, but which can also play a positive role. Montaigne, for instance, described this phenomenon as early as the sixteenth century (Montaigne, 1580/1981).

A good network also helps us to get and give strategic information, warnings, advice, factual help, protection, and feedback about our own performance and position. In this way, a social network is important for our perceived control over our position, environment, and future. This involves our own (informal) power position in the organization and the political complexities in that realm. This power position and its outcomes play an important part in the positive effects of social support on stress complaints. All in all, belonging to an effectively functioning network helps us to develop an optimal freedom of action, which enables us to focus on our work. But here, too, it is the case that when the social network becomes too important and time-consuming, this happens at the expense of our work.

Point for Reflection
How well embedded are the employees in your organization?

Sketch your own social network. Is it sufficiently extended over the different organizational levels and departments? Do you give sufficient time and attention to it?

How does the way you are embedded in your organization make you feel?

Safety

In order to function effectively and not to attract unnecessary attention, we have to experience our work environment as safe. This involves a variant of the 'basic trust', which every human being has to develop during the first years of life. People wouldn't be able to do anything if they worried about the safety of each muscular contraction contributing to that activity. We have to be able to believe in our general physical safety too. We can work better without having to worry about the collapse of the building, carcinogenic asbestos plates lining our air-conditioning system, unreliable electrical wiring, exploding geysers, and so on. This also applies to trusting our colleagues, managers, and subordinates: work becomes much more complicated when we know for sure that they are out to get us. Everything that goes wrong can unsettle our trust, for such events make us remember that we are less safe than we would want to be. This implies that, in order to feel safe, we must have worked through all our traumatic events from the past, such as an accident or a violent conflict, so that these do not continue to influence our present life.

We do not pay much attention to things that go well. At the same time, however, we develop a fascination for what goes wrong. This is demonstrated from the content of much of our conversation, as well as from the media, both fiction and non-fiction. What goes well is mainly a matter of mutual ethical agreements such as 'When I ask a question, you give an answer', 'When you pay, I deliver', and so on. These agreed principles are so self-evident that we only put them into words when something goes wrong. We do not expect that anybody wants to poison or swindle us. Apart from the fact that this makes it rather easy to poison or swindle us, it also means that our ethics are apparently very effective. If, for example, everybody lived according to the seven virtues and avoided the seven deadly sins, our safety would increase considerably, as is true with respect to many other ethical systems. The same applies to the way in which we acquire these ethics and allow them to rule our actions, for example by transferring them to our 'free will' (see Schabracq, 1991). The result is so self-evident that it feels more like biology than culture.

To return to work: in order to be able to work well, we should not be continually diverted by thoughts about danger, or warnings such as 'Pay attention', 'Look out', 'Behind you', or – even worse – the telling absence of these. For perceived or supposed danger interferes with the undivided attention needed for losing ourselves in our work. Conversely, too strong a preoccupation with safety can paralyse us so that it disturbs our work completely. In the building industry, for example, the safety prescriptions are sometimes ignored because following these prescriptions is thought to be 'too much work'.

Point for Reflection

How safe do you feel at work? To what degree do you trust your managers? To what degree do you trust your colleagues and your own staff?

What traumatic events have you experienced in the organization? What unpleasant events from the past are still not completely resolved?

Are there counterproductive prescriptions concerning safety? How does the safety in your organization make you feel?

Compatibility of values and goals

The compatibility of our personal values and convictions with those of the organizational culture is another crucial element of the effectiveness of a work environment. This compatibility is a central part of the 'person–environment' fit (P–E fit), an important concept in the Michigan stress model (Winnubst, De Jong & Schabracq, 1996). Only when there is a good fit between our environment and ourselves can we deal with our work in a self-evident way, without having to question everything that happens and that we do.

We are not continuously aware of our values and convictions and our goals in work. We are aware of them only when they are trampled on, or when it becomes impossible to achieve them, for instance as a result of changes in the organization or our work, or because of losing our job. When everything goes well, the compatibility of values and goals comes about organically. The organization selects people who are unlikely to oppose the existing values. By staying in the organization, they become even more socialized, almost automatically, while people who fail to fit in leave voluntarily or can be dismissed at the end of their probationary period (Schneider, 1987).

Problems occur only when one party (an employee or the organization) changes suddenly. For instance, by becoming a member of a radical sect, suffering from a stroke, or winning four million pounds in a lottery, employees can change so much that they can no longer bring themselves to do the same work. At the same time, an organization can change also, for example by a merger or reorganization, so that it no longer provides an appropriate environment for an employee. Table 2.3 describes some ideas and values about which employees and organizations can have strong differences of opinion, to such a degree that the differences can seriously hamper the effective functioning of the work environment.

Table 2.3 : Values and convictions

Without any claims to comprehensiveness, the following ideas can play a role in attuning ourselves to the organization. Primarily, this concerns both what we are allowed and made to do by ourselves and what we are allowed and made to do by the organization.

What is real and what 'does not exist' in the organization? And as a result of this: what are we allowed or compelled to react or not to react to, and what should we and shouldn't we take into account? And above all: do we want to take responsibility for all this?

A simple example is the existence of the hereafter and how we should deal with that in the organization. Other examples are believing or not believing in the existence of work stress, incompetence at high levels, the idea that a superior can be wrong, our own failure, need for help, emotionality in general, conflicts, unpleasant events from the past and their consequences. Essentially, this concerns the above-mentioned impossibilities, unthinkables, unspeakables, and blind spots. However, it is also about the fixed forms of everything in the organization.

What is good and what is bad in the organization? And do we want to subscribe to the consequences of it?

Does the organization deliberately expose employees to stress or other dangers? Does the organization demand from us that we act dishonestly, unjustly, dogmatically, unreliably, cruelly, greedily, or arrogantly? Conversely, does the organization have extremely high moral values that we find excessive? And do we want to work for an organization whose products or services we find despicable (an arms factory, a nuclear power plant, a cigarette manufacturer, a battery chicken farm, or a slaughterhouse)?

How does the organization treat its employees? Where does it stop for us?

Does the organization try to:
- keep us all employed;
- keep us healthy, free from stress and out of danger;
- pay us the highest possible wages;
- make us co-owners;
- make our work as pleasant as possible;
- feel responsible for our careers, education, and employability?

How does the organization deal with different groups of employees? And do we agree?
How do the career possibilities look for female employees (the 'glass ceiling')? How does the organization deal with different age groups, and with groups of different cultural and ethnic backgrounds? To what degree do stereotyping and prejudice from above play a role?

How are the employees expected to relate to each other in the organization? How formal is interaction? How much room is there for emotions? Is there any bullying of employees? Is there sexual harassment? Do employees go more or less their own way or does the organization lay emphasis on team-work? What role do personal relations play in decision making? To what degree does the organization rely on rules and job descriptions? Does the organization promote collaboration or does it encourage competition?

What degree of commitment and effort and what forms of productivity does the organization demand from us?

To what degree are your own values compatible with those of the organization?
- What are the main incompatibilities?
- How do you deal with these incompatibilities?

When formulating values and convictions, the organization is always the point of departure. However, when we are concerned with our own goals, we ourselves are the point of departure. Where this involves goals that we can achieve in our work, a good fit between organization and employee is of importance in order to keep the work environment functioning effectively. The more we can achieve our personal goals in our work, the more important it becomes to us, and the more likely it becomes that we can attain a state of flow in our work (see section 2.1 above).

Too great an emphasis on values or too narrow a focus on the achievement of goals can negatively affect efficiency of the work environment as well, by leading to various forms of overload. These go together with the disturbance of the balance between our work and our outside life (see the next section). Moreover, actually realizing our goals (in our work or elsewhere) might actually disappoint us.

Table 2.4 lists some frequently sought after goals, which may be possible outcomes of work. (Though the focus is different, there is some overlap in content with the values and convictions mentioned in Table 2.3.) Of course, different kinds of work provide different outcomes. So 'appropriate synchronization with the outside social and public environment' is not an outcome of working night shifts, while many temporary workers get considerably fewer outcomes on many of these aspects than their permanent colleagues.

Table 2.4: Possible goals or outcomes of work

Being able to support ourselves.

A certain lifestyle.

A contribution to our feelings of self-esteem and security.

A meaningful and active pastime.

Pleasure in the work itself.

Manufacturing complete and meaningful 'products'.

Personal development.

A clear perspective on the future, including progress in our career.

Status, prestige, power, and freedom, inside and outside the organization.

Valuable and pleasant contacts with others.

A clear temporal and spatial structure in our own life, including appropriate synchronization with the outside social and public environment.

Point for Reflection
Rank the importance of the different goals of Table 2.4 according to your own priorities. To what degree does the organization allow you to attain your most important goals? What improvements in this respect can and should be made?

Work as an autonomous domain

According to the rules of the 'golden mean', work must not determine our life too much or too little. When we are in work, a balance between the realms of work and our outside life is necessary. This implies that we have to manage the home–work interface by shielding off our work and outside life from each other sufficiently. When we are with our partner or our children, we should not have our minds on our work. Similarly, when we are working, our thoughts should not dwell too much on our partner and children. Because we are 'constructed' in such a way that we can only do one thing at a time, it is only by consciously doing this that we can perform optimally in our work and elsewhere. A related issue is that our work must be important enough to hold our attention. Essentially, this is the same story as that outlined in the previous section but with a different emphasis.

Point for Reflection
To *what degree are your work and private life well balanced?*

Suitable physical working conditions

Though physical working conditions are not directly the subject of this book, it is clear that they influence the effective functioning of the work environment. Physical dimensions include working conditions that are too noisy or too quiet, too cold or too hot, too wet or too dry, too dark or too light, having too much or too little air circulation, as well as the chemical composition of the air, and so on. In addition, it is about the availability of good equipment and tools, and a good fit between the equipment and tools and individual end-users – that is, the ergonomic characteristics of the work environment.

The work itself

Finally, the work itself determines to an important degree whether individuals can function effectively. Here too, the crucial question is: 'Can we keep our attention on the work in the right way?' Or in other words, 'Is the work challenging enough and can we handle the challenge?' Here too, the idea of a golden mean applies. This is principally a matter of the degree to which the work shows certain task characteristics. We will return to this in chapter 3, when we examine the separate stress sources. Here too, there are great individual differences, as illustrated by the different kinds of work mentioned in section 2.1.

2.4 STRESS

In the former two sections, we explored the profile of a daily life without stress, the existence of organizational culture, and the effective functioning of our work and work situation. In these accounts, the word stress hardly arose, but in this section we explain the meaning of the term.

Loss of control

When the everyday reality of our work environment is no longer functioning effectively – that is, when we cannot or do not want to keep our attention on our work sufficiently – the thinking processes steering our work become disorganized. We become unable to do our work well without damaging ourselves: either we just can't do it any more or we can't work ourselves up to doing it. If it were up to us, we would quit at that moment. This happens, for example, when we become overtired. In itself, this is not wrong at all, and it is not stress. We can stop working and have a rest. Later – for instance next day – we have probably recovered so well that we can keep our attention on our work again and can take it from there. Another example may be when the work situation leads to inefficiency, perhaps again because we are tired, or perhaps because our thoughts keep on wandering to other pressing work that should have been finished a long time ago. Whatever, we focus insufficiently on our work. The thinking processes steering our work are again disorganized considerably and threaten to go into disarray, but now we are obliged to do the same work for four more hours. In such a case, we are confronted by something that becomes increasingly difficult to handle. When we get irritated by this, it makes doing our work even more laborious. The same goes for the recurring thought of quitting the task, or better still, of giving up the stupid job altogether. In this way, we increasingly lose control over our work. As soon as such a situation ensues, we are confronted by stress.

Put more simply: when we can't and/or don't want to keep our attention on our work, but we have to do it anyway, this can evoke a stress reaction. Though work in itself is only a part of our life, the fact that our consciousness operates in such a way that we can do only one thing at a time means that our work is our life at that moment. Loss of control over our work thus becomes loss of control over our life at that moment, and that gives rise to a violent reaction.

Point for Reflection
Think of personal examples of occasions where you cannot and/or do not want to keep your attention on your work, but you have to do it anyway. How does it make you feel? What do you usually do about it?

The stress process

Stress at work stems from a basic emotional reaction (anger, fear, or anxiety) to the experience of a loss of control over our work, and therefore over our life and ourselves. We react as if we are in danger and our survival is at stake. These are global, all-or-nothing response patterns, with a radical physiological component, that are normally only appropriate for dealing with life-threatening situations. However, when these situations arise at our place of work, they are not usually life threatening.

The kind of situations we are talking about here concern factors in our work, our work environment, and aspects of ourselves, that lead to us being unable or unwilling to keep our attention on the task in hand. With regard to the factors that concern work and the work environment, often the problem is due to 'too much' or 'too little' of the same variables of which the optimum level makes our everyday life at work effective. Again, this is reliant upon achievable work, orderliness, social embedding, safety, compatibility of values and goals, no spillover to and from other areas of our life, and suitable physical working conditions. Concerning the third factor – aspects of ourselves – we can say that we suffer from stress when we move too far away from our most essential motives. This implies that we are then in a position of doing too few of the things that we are willing and able to do and too many of the things for which we are unwilling and/or unable. And above all, there is the obligation to get the job done. In chapter 3 section 2, we go more deeply into the specific sources of stress in our work and working environment. Anticipating section 3.2, in the next section we discuss an often-used distinction between various sources of work stress.

Underload and overload

The terms underload and overload are compatible with the idea of an effectively functioning middle region, in which the individual peculiarities of the person in question play an important part.

Underload

Underload occurs when we don't encounter enough challenge and meaning in our work. In other words, underload occurs when we have too little opportunity in our work to do the things that we like to do and that we are able to do well. This makes it increasingly hard for us to mobilize what is referred to as sufficient processing capacity. Our attention slips away. We become less alert. This results in us having to force ourselves more and more to keep our attention on our work, which is becoming increasingly hard to do, with the result that control over our work becomes problematic. We experience work as unengaging, and the associated feelings experienced vary from boredom, alienation, and drowsiness, to the absence of any feeling at all.

Point for Reflection
What kinds of underload do you see in your environment? How do those involved cope with these forms of underload?

What kinds of underload do you know from your own experience? How did you deal with them?

Overload

Overload occurs when the challenge of work is too great. In other words, overload occurs when we have to do too many things at work that we do not like or are not able to do well. Our attention jumps from one thing to another, without getting any grip on what happens. We find ourselves in a state of chaos, and control over our work has become impossible.

Point for Reflection
What kinds of overload do you see in your environment? How do people cope with these forms of overload?

What kinds of overload do you know from your own experience? How did you deal with them?

Overload and underload usually occur only after having done the same work for some time. Combinations of overload and underload occur frequently – for example, a great deal of meaningless work – and these are considered to be extra harmful to our well-being and health (Karasek and Theorell, 1990).

Point for Reflection
Where in your organization do combinations of overload and underload occur? What kinds of effects does this bring about? What can be done about it?

Actually, it is not completely clear to us to what degree overload and underload are essentially different phenomena. For, in both cases, the common final path is loss of control and an emotional reaction to that. We are tempted to think, however, that the case of underload is foremost a matter of the second stage of the stress process, while overload is more strongly connected to the primary stage (these stages are described in the next subsection). The logical consequence of this would be that overload eventually turns into underload, for example because of the fact that we ignore the problems and withdraw ourselves, emotionally and cognitively, from the chaos of our work.

The stages of a stress process

Based on a series of somewhat gruesome animal experiments, Selye (1956) distinguished three stages in a complete stress process, which he called the 'general adaptation syndrome' (GAS).

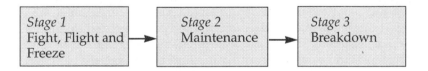

Figure 2.1: The stages of a stress process

The fact that we share these reaction patterns with other animals implies that they are not responses necessarily attuned to the subtleties of our everyday life and work (Sapolsky, 1994). In order to describe the stress process in more detail, we review the three stages below (freely adapted from Selye, 1956). Of course, the stages overlap at some points. Moreover, there is a considerable individual variation in the content of the three stages, particularly where it concerns specific emotions, experiences, and complaints.

Stage 1: fight, flight and freeze

First, there are the reaction patterns that we can describe as fight (linked to anger), flight (linked to fear), and freezing (linked to fright) – the three f-reactions described by Cannon (1935). The rationale behind fight and flight is obvious. A danger or threat has appeared and we have to eliminate it or escape from it. The accompanying physiological changes prepare our body for the great effort needed for that. This involves chemical changes in our nerves and an increased production of hormones by the adrenal medulla (adrenaline and noradrenaline), that bring about changes in the energy supply to the body. This reveals itself in raised blood pressure, a faster heartbeat, a higher blood sugar level, a higher muscle tone, and faster breathing. In this way, the body mobilizes resources in order to be able to proceed to powerful, explosive activity.

Freezing shows the same rapid mobilization of the body to great activity, but because of the fact that we do not act immediately, we provide ourselves with the freedom to gather more information in order to be able to reach a better decision. In addition, the resulting immobility makes some animals less conspicuous, which may have definite survival value.

Usually, a form of freezing, mostly in the weakened form of an orientation response, precedes one of the two other basic reactions. An explanation is that fight and flight can result in high costs, such as being wounded or dying or loss of territory. In Russian psychology (Razran, 1964), the orientation response is characterized as the beginning – in an evolutionary sense – of thinking. An orientation response is a reaction to a new or unexpected phenomenon. This reaction implies a suspension of what we are doing and experiencing, and sharpens our senses. All attention is focused on the phenomenon that brought about the reaction and we orient ourselves physically to the phenomenon, hence the reaction's name.

When we assess the phenomenon in question as important and disturbing, we can then try to cope with it. When coping is successful, or when the orientation response turns out to be a false alarm, we usually try to get back to our original task. Often, this is not easy to do, partly because a suddenly interrupted task provides few cues for taking it up again at the right point, partly also because the heightened activation interferes with task performance, while it takes some time to undo the increase in activity levels. The frequent occurrence of orientation responses can lead in this way to serious task disturbances, especially when tasks demand a lot of precision and attention. In this way, frequent orientation reactions can be a source of stress and alienation, for example for people who are in a situation that, to them, is new or unsafe.

The nature and extremity of the f-reactions depend, of course, on the events and the person in question. As mentioned, the three f-reactions enable the body to attempt to counteract acute, life-threatening events. Though these primitive mammalian reactions may be appropriate for situations of life or death, they are usually unacceptable at work: freezing in fright, kicking or biting our manager, or running away are all considered inappropriate (Sapolsky, 1994). So we have to suppress those reactions. This requires extra attention and effort, while the bodily arousal that accompanies the original reaction stays at the same level, in situations that are sometimes really problematic and threatening. It becomes even more difficult to deal with these situations in a satisfying way. Moreover, the heightened activation means that we have difficulty in calming down and may experience sleep problems. At the same time, the normal 'maintenance and recovery' processes (digestion, tissue 'repair', etc.) are suspended.

Point for Reflection
What typically makes you angry? How does it feel? How do you deal with it?

When do you actually flee? Do you remember any instances when you wanted to disappear altogether?

What occasions do you avoid? How do these different situations feel?

Stage 2: maintenance

When, in the short term, we do not succeed in removing or neutralizing the causes of the decreased effectiveness of the work situation – that is, the reason that we can't keep our attention on our work – the second stage of the stress process has started. Stress has become a 'normal' aspect of our existence, which we often do not even recognize as such. Work is still troublesome, but we carry on. We deny the unpleasant character of the situation. There is not much feeling at all. We work around the disturbing factors as much as possible. Sometimes, some irritation, or another violent feeling, flares up, but most of the time we feel nothing at all. Our world has become smaller; we do not experience much. It is as if we have escaped from a lion by running to a tree and climbing up it, and we are now trying to make our life as comfortable as possible on an uncomfortable branch. We would rather forget the fact that the lion is lying down there, looking at us.

In the second stage, hormones play a part also, namely those of the hypothalamus (ACTH) and adrenal cortex (the glycocorticosteroids). We still live on our reserves and neglect our bodily recovery and maintenance functions. In time, this stage passes gradually and without being noticed into the third stage – breakdown – at least as long as the stress sources remain active. The second stage is characterized by the gradual disappearance of positive, motivating feelings, including such feelings towards others. So the kinds of learning and development based on need gratification and reward disappear also, a state called 'anhedonia' (Willner, 1993). Often, this is accompanied by feelings of alienation or depression. We avoid social contacts, and – when we still interact with others – we behave in a more impersonal way than people expect of us. This interferes with our social relations and this, in turn, results in a decrease in the potential positive outcomes, the emotional support and the rewards of our informal power position. Lastly, our immune system starts to function less well and we gradually become more liable to illnesses.

Point for Reflection
Do you recognize this maintenance stage in your environment? What are your own experiences with this maintenance stage? How would you describe the feelings associated with it?

Stage 3: breakdown
In the last stage – and, fortunately, most of the time, it does not come to that – the hormone production of the adrenal cortex and medulla comes to a halt and our performance breaks down completely. In terms of our lion example: we lose it and fall from our branch. We are completely exhausted and working is out of the question. We risk a serious illness and may even die. We call this state 'nervous breakdown' or 'burnout' (though these terms are used rather indiscriminately). Recovery usually takes a very long time. Japan has witnessed the phenomenon of 'kiroshi': sudden death by a cardiac arrest caused by excessive overwork and stress, and a life that is completely out of balance.

All in all, work stress is a simple concept on the one hand: an emotional process activated by the loss of control over work that we have to do. On the other hand, it is an extremely complicated concept, because the causes behind the loss of control, and also those behind the obligation to finish our work, consist of ever-changing interactions of work, work environment, and the individual.

Point for Reflection
What do you know about the breakdown stage from other people around you? What was its most striking feature? What do you know from your own experience?

Stress and effort

An important, though maybe superfluous, point is that stress is something other than effort, tension, or high activation *per se*. Unlike stress, effort and tension do not have to be associated with failing control, nor with unpleasant feelings and undesired effects on sense making and health. Continuous effort and high activation, however, can eventually lead to stress, and this in fact often happens. Many people, however, like such a way of working. It is the only way they can feel they are really working and that enhances their feelings of pride and self-esteem. Though most of us do not like stress and exhaustion at all, such a state can be a reason to look at oneself with some pleasure and pride. Some of us exploit it in order to claim attention and care from our partners ('You know how hard I've worked this week'). And when that is not successful, we can always surrender to a pleasant form of self-pity. Another point is that the fantasy of being able to bear anything may sometimes be very attractive, even when it can be described as a form of masochism.

Point for Reflection
How attractive is working too hard to you?

Physical and mental workload

A last issue we want to deal with in this section is the difference between physical and mental workload in relation to stress. During the last decades, a major shift has occurred from physical to mental workload. Though heavy physical work can be taxing, it does not by itself evoke stress. Hard physical work also implies a form of physical exercise and does not usually lead to exhaustion, at least not in our Western world. We become tired, take a rest, and recover. Hard physical labour is also characterized by more 'natural' pauses. Moreover, such work enables us to work off tension and usually does not give rise to sleeping difficulties from worrying. Our governments may actually have a point in their campaigns to encourage people to take more exercise.

A heavy mental workload, without much physical effort or movement, is much more likely to give rise to stress. Apart from the absence of physical exercise, this is a result of the fact that we are, biologically speaking, not very well adapted to this kind of activity. When we put in a great amount of mental effort, our physiology acts as if we have put in a great physical effort, with all the undesired effects that we have described in this section. However the absence of the accompanying physiological activity means that often these high levels of hormonal activation have no actual release. This can have serious implications for the well-being of the individual if this builds up over a period of time

Point for Reflection
Is your workload mainly mental or mainly physical in nature? What consequences does that have or should that have for your personal stress management?

All in all, the shift from physical to mental workload is probably an important factor in the growing prominence of stress and stress-related complaints.

3. Stress reactions and stress sources

While the former chapter addressed the key question 'What is stress?', here we search for answers to the more concrete questions: 'What do our reactions to stress look like?' and 'What stress sources are found in work situations?' An important objective of the chapter is to give you the opportunity to apply its content as much as possible to your own personal situation and your own work organization. A number of checklists are included to map both reactions to, and sources of, stress.

Point for Reflection
Which stress reactions and stress sources do you recognize as ones that you experience?

Which ones are experienced by your colleagues and managers? Where and when do they occur?

It is a good exercise to rank the stress reactions and sources in terms of their importance and relevance. In this way, both you and your colleagues can determine your own personal top five stress reactions and sources, and so rank the main stress sources for your department and organization.

3.1 INDIVIDUAL STRESS REACTIONS

Introduction

Stress researchers have described a great number of diverse stress reactions, most of which are experienced as unpleasant. These reactions make us less effective and efficient, as well as less creative and open to learning. However, such reactions are not exclusively related to stress. They can also be symptoms of alcoholism, menopause, premenstrual syndrome, sick-building syndrome, midlife crisis, the grief process, and so on. Some of these reactions can be classified as 'vague complaints', that is, complaints that medical practitioners do not associate with a clear physical cause or therapy, and which they classify as 'psychological'.

Some reactions obviously stem from the reaction patterns of the first stress stage outlined in the previous chapter. (For a survey of reactions based on these patterns, see Bernstein & Craft-Rozen, 1989.) Other reactions are more easily associated with the passive acceptance of a stress source, as well as the denial of stage 2. Still other reactions cannot be unambiguously linked to any stage. We distinguish between the following kinds of stress reactions: changes in thinking; fight elements; tension; loss of pleasure and motivation; physical complaints and illnesses.

Changes in thinking

Many changes in thinking can be described as an exaggeration of our most characteristic ways of functioning: these consist of 'too much' of what are essentially our strongest points. Such reactions can be described as our personal pitfalls (see section 4.1). Being exaggerated, these stress reactions are often not very well attuned to situational demands, and so can be irritating to the people around us. Many of these reactions are characterized as 'primitive' or 'overreacting'. We sometimes even experience this as regressing to ways of functioning that we associate with our past. Moreover, these changed ways of thinking tend to imply a loss of creativity. Though these changes are typical stress reactions, we often do not experience them as such, but as familiar ways of functioning. They are not in themselves unpleasant: they do not evoke much feeling in us at all. Moreover, we sometimes use these thoughts to collect 'evidence' to justify our emotional reactions: 'You see, I'm right!'.

Another important point here is that we should recognize these reactions for what they are: too much of an intrinsically positive quality. This can help us to deal with other people who show these kinds of changed thinking. By interpreting their annoying ways of thinking as being too much of something good, we can find the right buttons to make them less annoying: 'Of course you only want to…, but right now…').

Self-Assessment Questionnaire – 3

Changed Ways of Thinking Checklist

Place a cross (X) in the 'Yes' column for each change of thinking that is a characteristic way in which you react to stress.

Changed ways of thinking	*Yes*
Focusing on errors and wrongs	___
Dogmatism	___
Focusing too exclusively on the one correct procedure	___
Inflated sense of own importance in solving a certain problem	___
Focusing too exclusively on self-interest	___
Inability to distinguish between main and side issues	___
Taking refuge in quick solutions, outward appearances and, ultimately, deception	___
Being too flexible and not conscientious enough	___
Being too much like a chameleon with different kinds of people	___
Bad temper	___
Excessive avoidance of routine activities	___
Foolhardiness and taking needless risks	___
Economizing and stinginess	___
Retreating into an ivory tower when action is called for	___
Intellectualizing	___
Mind reading and suspicion	___
Procrastination	___
Indecisiveness and doubt	___
Being overenthusiastic about new options	___
Starting up too many projects	___
Running away from responsibilities	___
Thinking in black and white, and generalizing from isolated incidents	___
Stereotypical thinking	___
Concluding too quickly	___
Thoughts that keep wandering; mentally falling asleep	___
Giving in too easily and being too nice	___
Diminished creativity	___
Other processing failures	___
Problems with concentrating and attending	___
Interfering thoughts	___
Not being able to take in new information	___
Thinking blocks	___
Blind spots	___
Forgetfulness	___
Narrowing of attention	___
Low perceived competence	___

Fight elements

Fight elements are derived from the fight response that can be characteristic of the first stress stage and the hostile or impersonal behaviour that may occur in the second stage. The latter then serves as a kind of defence against other people's claims on our attention. Examples of fight elements are feelings of anger and irritation, and exhibiting the behavioural elements associated with these emotions. Another example is a heightened sense of territoriality, which we often experience in work situations. This is revealed in a need for more control over our environment, a lowered threshold for interpreting something as an intrusion, and unexpectedly fierce defensive reactions. This territoriality is not a purely physical matter, but pertains also to our rights, privileges, and claims. The increased need for control expresses itself in being easily distracted and violently irritated by the behaviour of other people in our immediate environment (talking, smoking, restlessness), and being irritated by traces and signs of their presence (a coat over a chair, dirty coffee cups and ashtrays, litter and stains). Though being angry may actually feel rather good, it obviously interferes with our ability to function smoothly in a working context.

Self-Assessment Questionnaire – 4

Fight Elements Checklist

Place a cross (X) in the 'Yes' column for each fight element that is typically characteristic of you when reacting to stress.

Fight Elements	*Yes*
Feeling angry	____
Feeling irritated	____
Disliking one or more persons intensely	____
Blaming others	____
Fierce verbal reactions	____
Biting sarcasm	____
Feeling crowded by other people	____
Being excessively distracted by noise	____
Being excessively distracted by smell	____
Being involved in conflicts	____

Feeling dissatisfied	—
Taking unnecessary risks and being involved in accidents	—
Disturbed relationships with other people	—
Tense shoulders	—
Clenched fists	—
Kicking movements	—
Sniffing loudly	—
Engaging in staring contests	—
Being irritated by traces of other people's presence	—
Frowning	—
Clenched jaw	—

Tension

Tension is another characteristic reaction of the first stress stage. It can be a manifestation of the freezing response, but it may also be a suppression of a fight or flight response. In some people, tension is also part of the second stage of a stress process.

Self-Assessment Questionnaire – 5

Tension Checklist

Place a cross (X) in the 'Yes' column for each form of tension that is typically characteristic of you when reacting to stress.

Form of tension	Yes
Restlessness	
Working uncoordinatedly	—
Agitation	—
Hurry	—
Concentration problems	—
Perspiring when it is not very hot	—
Worrying	—
Going over and over the same line of thought	—
Compulsive behaviour	—
Heavy smoking	—
High alcohol use	—
Stumbling	—
Bumping into things	—

Restless foot movements	——
Drumming one's fingers	——
Fiddling with objects	——
Overstretching one's hands	——
Overstretching one's feet	——
Holding one's breath	——
Fiddling with one's body	——
Rigid bodily posture	——
Shiftiness	——

Loss of pleasure and motivation

Loss of pleasure and motivation is principally part of the second and third stress stage. This implies that these stress reactions are more severe than those that we have dealt with previously. Somebody who is suffering from these reactions has reached a more advanced stage in their stress process.

Self –Assessment Questionnaire – 6

Loss of Pleasure and Motivation Checklist

Place a cross (X) in the 'Yes' column for each form of loss of pleasure and motivation that is typically characteristic of you when reacting to stress.

Form of pleasure and motivation loss	Yes
Apathy	——
Loss of interest	——
Boredom	——
Loss of involvement	——
Reluctance to experience anything new	——
Sighing	—
Avoiding social contacts	——
Dejection	——
Hypersensitivity	——
Loss of appetite	——
Alienation	——
Shame	——
Insecurity	——
Fatigue	——
Depression	——

Physical complaints and illnesses

Most physiological and other bodily stress reactions are primarily manifestations of a high activation level, and are indications of an advanced stress process. The reactions listed in Questionnaire 7 are mentioned frequently by those at this particular stage.

Self-Assessment Questionnaire – 7

Bodily Complaints Checklist

Place a cross (X) in the 'Yes' column for each bodily complaint that is typically characteristic of you when reacting to stress.

Bodily complaint	Yes
Hot flushes	—
Dry mouth	—
Dry skin	—
Hyperventilation (breathing too quickly)	—
Nausea	—
Problems with falling asleep	—
Problems with sleeping through the night	—
Sexual malfunctioning	—
Palpitations	—
Headache	—
Lower back pain	—
Dizziness	—
Fainting	—
Seeing stars or spots	—

In the longer term, these reactions can lead or contribute to more severe physical disorders. So stress can exacerbate or contribute to the disorders listed in Questionnaire 8.

Self-Assessment Questionnaire – 8

Illnesses Checklist

Place a cross (X) in the 'Yes' column for each illness that has been experienced by you as a reaction to stress.

Disorder	Yes
Exhaustion, burnout, and ME	___
Repetitive strain injury	___
Stomach complaints (stomach ulcers and bleeding)	___
Intestinal complaints	___
Skin complaints (eczema, acne)	___
High blood pressure	___
Brain infarct	___
Inflammations	___
Persistent colds and flu	___
Cardiac complaints (heart infarct, rhythm disturbances)	___
Lung complaints (asthma, bronchitis, pneumonia)	___
Infectious diseases in general	___
Cancer	___

Stress reactions as sources of stress

Stress reactions usually make it more difficult to do our work easily, and so contribute to a decrease in our ability to function effectively with regard to our work and work environment.

People generally consider stress reactions to be inappropriate or abnormal. They can disturb the normal course of events and evoke colleagues' disapproval, irritation, and avoidance, which can make it even more difficult to keep our attention on our work in the right way. Moreover, none of these reactions contributes anything to our effectiveness at work: stress reactions rarely take away stress sources. Lastly, our efforts in trying to subdue these reactions are usually at the expense of our available attention, without resulting in anything positive. Given that stress reactions generally lead to a limitation of the degree to which we are able to keep our attention on our work, we can consider stress reactions as a source of stress in their own right. A stress process therefore can be cyclical and self-perpetuating.

3.2 SOURCES OF STRESS

What do we mean by a source of stress?

In our work, a stress source is something or someone that interferes with the division of attention needed for the work that we have to do. When this interference significantly diminishes control over our work, and consequently over our life, a stress process is activated. So anything that prevents us from attending to the work that we have to do may be a source of stress. Essentially, stress sources bring about a form of powerlessness: we lack sufficient coping techniques to deal with the situation in a self-evident and easy way.

In this section, we examine sources of stress inherent in the work environment and the work itself, and classify stressors as too much or too little of certain qualities. For the work environment, we make use of five of the six qualities described in section 2.3 as necessary conditions for effective functioning in the work environment (we do not discuss physical work circumstances here), namely: orderliness; social embedding; safety; compatibility of values, convictions, and goals; work as an independent life realm.

Concerning the work itself, we deal with only one quality, namely the challenges it affords. And here again, we are concerned with 'too much' or 'too little'. Of course, stress sources from several categories can occur within one organization at the same time.

Too little orderliness

Too little orderliness may well be the best known form of stress: all kinds of issues fighting for our attention, making it almost impossible to attend to a single issue. In such a situation, we are supposed to keep all the loose ends in our head, in order to get back to them when we get the chance, while many tracks turn out to be dead ends. Furthermore, we often have to deal with strong emotions, as well as with ambiguous and inconsistent cues and behaviours that can set us on the wrong track. Some people just love and thrive on all of this and perform better when faced with such a challenge. To others, work degenerates into an endless succession of daily hassles.

Too little orderliness is common in all kinds of professional firms: stock exchanges, dealer rooms of merchant banks, advertising agencies, and in the media. Too little orderliness shows a considerable overlap with the category 'tasks that imply too much challenge', which is dealt with later on in this chapter. It may have very diverse causes, which can reinforce each other. Some of these causes are out-lined below.

A turbulent environment

A turbulent, rapidly changing, or competitive organizational envi-ronment, which continually demands fast actions and reactions, is often found in a news or dealer room. In this situation, we constantly have to deal with more than one issue at a time.

'Modelling' and 'emotional contagion'

Emotional contagion from colleagues who show a high level of excitement and stress is also often found in a news or dealer room. Deviating activation levels of people around us have been proved to be very contagious. So an agitated person can spread commotion, while a depressive person may have a paralysing effect on others. This process tends to takes place in a more or less automatic way without many conscious choices on our behalf (Schabracq, 1987; Hatfield, Cacioppo, & Rapson, 1994).

A new or fast-growing organization

A young organization in its first stage where everybody still does everything, or a rapidly growing organization, often have a lack of structure, standard procedures, and specialized well-trained employees. Consequentially, everybody is terribly busy reinventing the wheel, while the pace at which things get done is often much slower than seems reasonable.

High turnover

In an organization with high levels of sick leave, turnover, or a high proportion of employees on temporary contracts, those employees with longer tenure are often busy breaking in new people. As they hardly have time left to do their own work, this has an adverse cumulative effect. Moreover, many of the newly trained employees leave after a short time, which does not make the efforts of the estab-lished workforce more rewarding and meaningful. Also, in an orga-nization with high sick leave and turnover, more things tend to go wrong: high sick leave and turnover can be considered to be a case of choosing with one's feet.

Working with many different people

Working in different and frequently changing teams of very diverse people, with differing priorities and competencies, and diverse cultural and ethnic backgrounds is common to people working in a matrix organization, as well as to everyone who works in multinational and cross-cultural environments. An extreme example would be that of too much foreign travel.

Reorganizations or mergers

Reorganizations and mergers, especially when they happen in quick succession, often bring about all kind of changes in jobs and departments, and may lead to early retirements and redundancies. These changes are a collective process that can evoke strong and highly contagious emotions. This happens not only because we have to abandon a familiar way of functioning, but also because there is uncertainty about how things will turn out, which gives rise to rumours. Organizational changes often imply radical intrusions on individual practices and can ultimately lead to increased stress. In addition, such changes tend to happen in rapid sucession, change on change, which does not improve employees' motivation or ability to adapt.

Self-Assessment Questionnaire – 9

Too Little Orderliness Checklist

Place a cross (X) in the 'Yes' column for each form of too little orderliness that is a source of stress for you.

Consequences of too little orderliness	*Yes*
Many things going wrong	____
Appointments that cannot be kept	____
Lots of demands for immediate action	____
Doing several things at the same time	____
Having to do tasks that interfere with each other	____
All kinds of issues fighting for our attention	____
Having to keep in mind all kinds of unfinished business	____
Much communication with many people	____

Having to spend much time instructing others	—
Working with different people all the time	—
Stressed colleagues	—
Sudden emotional outbursts	—
High absenteeism	—
High turnover	—
Many temporary employees	—
Causes of too little orderliness	Yes
Reorganization	—
Merger	—
A turbulent and quickly changing organizational environment	—
A competitive organizational environment	—
Changes in jobs	—
Introduction of new computer programs	—
New managers	—
A quickly growing organization	—
A young organization	—
Many new employees	—

Too much emphasis on orderliness

When orderliness becomes a goal in itself, it can obscure other goals. Sticking to time-consuming formal procedures, checks, and double checks leads to a limitation of what we are allowed to do. In this way, it may interfere with work being carried out effectively and efficiently. This results in an ineffective and inefficient way of working which surfaces, for example, in problems of internal and external communication, 'political' relationships, slow decision making, and stagnation of projects. These problems present themselves as unchangeable data, ruled by relentless and indifferent natural laws, and are characteristic of bureaucracies.

People working in such organizations develop a good eye for rank, status symbols, movements up and down, and the possibilities and dangers that these imply. There is much political jargon, of a somewhat legalistic nature, with many words with abstract meanings. This is the language use of a permanent conspiracy, with its inherent suspicion and fear of outsiders, the result of too much orderliness making it impossible to deal with issues in a straightforward manner.

When outsiders ask an employee of a bureaucratic organization – with whom they relate quite well privately – a factual question about their work, the outsider often experiences a kind of *'praecox Gefühl'*. This term stems from pre-war psychiatry and refers to a feeling of something essentially alien, which makes it impossible to relate to. This feeling was used as an indication that the other person was suffering from 'dementia praecox', or schizophrenia, as it is now called.

At an individual level, too much orderliness leads to hiding emotions, denial of problems, and conflicts stemming from annoying incidents in the past. It is characterized by a ritual way of working, concentrating on following particular conventions, without paying attention to – or even disdaining – outcomes and results. Moreover, many colleagues are bored and will not take any risks, but still want everything to go their way, and such a system offers many possibilities for this. Many people, however, eventually cannot stand this way of working. They complain about high workload and many suffer from alienation and stress.

All this is common in big bureaucratic organizations, such as ministries and other public and semi-public organizations, but also in multinational companies and other organizations with a rigid hierarchy, such as military or paramilitary organizations and some churches. The causes are obvious: too many rules and too strict a hierarchy with very precisely delineated communication lines and responsibilities. This style is typical of a well-established culture, which has much to offer to people who reach the top when it comes to power (status, prestige, influence), certainty, and, in some cases, money.

Self-Assessment Questionnaire –10

Too Much Orderliness Checklist

Place a cross (X) in the 'Yes' column for each of the possible responses to an overemphasis on orderliness that is a source of stress to you.

Consequences of too much emphasis on orderliness	Yes
The feeling that you cannot get anything done	___
Too many rules	___
Too strict a hierarchy	___
Too rigid job descriptions	___

Having to get approval from too many people to get anything done	——
Colleagues who are excessively afraid to make a bad impression	——
Too precisely delineated communication lines	——
Colleagues who just go through the moves	——
A very political climate	——
A taboo on emotionalism	——
Suspicion of strangers	——
Denial of problems	——
Emphasis on conventional conduct	——
Orderliness as a goal in itself	——
Colleagues who do not want to take any risks	——
A very formal way of working	——

Too little social embedding

As mentioned before (in sections 2.1 and 2.3), for many people social contact at work is the main reason for coming to work every day. The sudden loss of those contacts can hit hard, and can even be a life event (see section 2.1), a matter that unsettles our fixed ways of doing things and paying attention, and demands a new adaptation from us. As such, it can be a source of stress in its own right. The causes are self-evident: either we ourselves or others can leave our jobs. And social isolation in itself is to many people a source of stress, certainly to an extraverted person. We lack social support from others and have to manage without the outcomes of our informal power position described in 2.3. This can often undermine an effective work situation considerably. Social isolation can have different causes. Here, we describe a number of these causes as sources of stress.

Role transitions
Examples of role transitions are coming into an organization, change of job, and leaving the organization, either to go to another organization or by retirement or work disability. These different transitions can differ greatly in the degree to which they evoke stress. However, in all these cases, we have to leave a position within a social network and sometimes also the network itself. The pain of such a departure often depends on the degree to which the transition is voluntary. Lay-

off and work disability, as involuntary transitions, can be very traumatic, while retirement is a mixed blessing. Another important factor is the character of the new role. In most cases, the problems of taking on a new role or job are more a matter of a (temporary) lack of orderliness.

Losing colleagues

Losing colleagues happens primarily to older employees who have worked in an organization for a long time. The people who hired them, their patrons and sponsors, have left a long time ago. Gradually, almost all their favourite, familiar colleagues, superiors, assistants, and outside contacts also disappear for various reasons: replacement, leaving to join another organization, lay-off, accidents, retirement, and death. It leaves them with an impoverished social network, because they are often not inclined to actively fill up the empty spaces. Older people are often more reserved than younger ones in this respect: 'Getting to know people is something that just happens, not something you do' (Schabracq & Winnubst, 1996b).

Massive lay-offs

When an organization decides to slim down – which has happened often during recent years – and lays off many employees, those who stay behind experience the problems mentioned above to an intensified degree. Moreover, such a course of affairs can lead to feelings of unpleasantness and guilt for those who stay ('what have we done to still be working here?'). Moreover, there is a good chance that many of the people who stay will lose their trust in the organization, especially when it comes to its future intentions ('You ask yourself, will I be next?'). This influences employees' commitment and motivation. This so-called 'survivors' syndrome' is probably also a matter of too much insecurity.

Physical barriers which impede social contact

Physical barriers, stemming from the organization of production and the work itself, can cause social isolation. The lonely position of a crane driver provides a good example. Another example is the work cubicle, which has become widely known from the Dilbert strips. Especially in simple work – in which personal contacts can actually make an important contribution to work satisfaction – such physical hindrances can make for an often unnecessary source of stress.

Being lonely at the top

Social isolation at the top of the organization is a serious problem. Apart from being a stress source for the manager in question, it harms the quality of communication. This applies to bottom-up communication ('The management hasn't a clue about what we're doing here and it seems a good idea to keep it that way') as well as top-down communication ('Some things you can't explain to them; they just don't get it'). Here, the quality of leadership and management are at stake.

The causes differ. On the one hand, there is the idea that it is impossible to interact in an open and personal way with employees because of their possible hidden agendas and intentions. Often, this is a kind of defence against the greater attention that employees pay to their manager, which we deal with in the next section under the heading of 'Unbalanced social exchange, getting more than we give'. On the other hand, employees tend to feel fearful and unwelcome. Moreover, groups that don't have compatible interests often perceive each other in a distorted way and entertain prejudices and stereotypes about each other. Lastly, both parties can usually improve their social skills considerably.

This kind of poor communication and poor management is a very important source of stress in everyday working life. Something similar may occur in communication between departments or teams, though this usually causes less stress. When interdependent departments do not communicate well with each other, this can lead, for example, to unpredictable fluctuations in the stream of work, resulting in all kinds of unexpected temporary task overload and underload.

A climate of distrust and conflict

This results in contacts remaining limited to the few people we trust, so that life becomes rather isolated. Such a climate can also be characterized as one with an insufficient sense of safety. A similar outcome may be the consequence of an organization characterized by too much orderliness.

Self-Assessment Questionnaire – 11

Too Little Social Embedding Checklist

Place a cross (X) in the 'Yes' column for each cause of too little social embedding that may be a source of stress for you.

Cause of too little social embedding	Yes
Impossibility of communication due to noise	___
Physical barriers which impede social contact	___
A physically isolated position	___
Losing colleagues	___
A climate of distrust	___
A climate of hidden conflicts	___
Insufficient feedback about performance	___
Being much older than your colleagues and executives	___
Being lonely at the top of a department or organization	___
Too little appreciation from executives	___
An executive with insufficient social skills	___
Poor or too little communication between management and work site	___
Poor or too little communication between departments	___
Too impersonal an atmosphere	___

Too much social embedding

Our social embedding can cause undesired effects in several ways. For instance, there are territorial infringements, sexual harassment, and conflicts, which can all affect our sense of safety, which is why we deal with these in the next section. There are also the more chronic forms of embedding that are too intense or undesired, which is what this section is about. We look here at lack of privacy, an organizational culture focusing strongly on the private realm, and work in which the balance between getting and giving has been disturbed, because people get much more than they give.

Lack of privacy

Different cultures deal differently with privacy. Some do not even have knowledge of the concept. However, in a culture that invented the concept of privacy, the open-plan office is a strange perversion: a huge room filled with people who can all see each other, and who can also phone and e-mail each other, during a large part of their waking existence. Some people are dedicated devotees, but that is only normal with perversions. To others, however, it results in a totally unacceptable work environment. From this perspective, Dilbert's cubicles (see the former section) would be welcome. But the open-plan office is only one example. Essentially, this applies to every work environment that exposes us too defencelessly to the supervision of our executives and the perception of others in general.

A culture that is too person-oriented
In some organizational cultures, it is usual to share all life's joys and sorrows with each other, both work-related and private. This can make it hard to keep one's mind on one's work. Stress may be a result especially when the stories are very harrowing, we happen to be very busy, or when failing to pay attention to our colleagues is interpreted as an unkind lack of interest. This kind of situation frequently occurs, for example, in social work and nursing organizations.

Unbalanced social exchange – getting more than we give
We find examples of this kind of unbalanced social exchange in almost all situations where 'stars' exist. Stars are people who attract much attention and emotion, sometimes through the media. As a result, their everyday reality has become much larger than life while, as human beings, they can only cope with a human life of a normal size. For many of them, this dilemma interferes with the manage-ability of their everyday work situations, especially when they derive their star status from their work. This happens most often when they themselves have come to believe in their extraordinary status, which is more likely to happen when their self-esteem has not been well developed or has been damaged. This variant of unbalance is an important theme in world literature (the Greek dramas, Shakespeare, etc.) as well as in the popular media. In spite of the efforts of many religions and their saints and savants, 'something for nothing' and 'what happened next' remain themes that stimulate our imagination probably more than the reverse form of exchange unbalance, giving more than we get. We shall deal with the latter form of unbalance under the heading of 'Too much compatibility of values and goals'.

Self-Assessment Questionnaire – 12

Too Much Social Embedding Checklist

Place a cross (X) in the 'Yes' column for each form of too much social embedding that is a source of stress for you.

Form of too much social embedding	*Yes*
Lack of privacy	——
Too personal an atmosphere	——
Having to listen too much to private, emotional stories	——
Attracting too much attention and emotion	——
Being exposed to other persons constantly	——
Feedback about performance that is too extensive, brief, or directive	——
Being surrounded by emotional colleagues	——

Too little safety

In order not to have our attention diverted unnecessarily, we have to experience our work environment as safe. Perceived danger makes it difficult to keep our mind on our work and so is a source of stress. We discuss some of the causes below.

Traumatic experiences at work

Traumatic experiences are life-threatening events or events that imply a gross violation of our personal integrity (assault, rape, or robbery). Frequently occurring examples at work are hold-ups, accidents, and client aggression. Such events can completely unsettle our trust in the safety of our work environment. Apart from the risk of ending up in a depressive state when we fail to work through these experiences adequately, it can also result in events that are harmless in themselves evoking violent stress reactions. An example might be when some suspicious looking – but actually innocent – people come into a bank that has already been robbed twice.

Insecurity

The feeling of insecurity can be brought about by anything that undermines one's present sense of security. Examples are: intimidation; sexual harassment; serving as a scapegoat; confrontations with malicious or unreliable colleagues and bosses. Concerning the last point, we want to emphasize that real psychopaths are quite often found in organizations. By psychopaths, we mean people who use other people mercilessly, and then disappear to another organization when there is nothing left to take or when things get too hot for them.

A feeling of insecurity can also stem from painful events that have happened at work in the past. Though these events may be of a different scale to the traumatic events mentioned above, their causes lie in the organization and may unsettle our trust in the organization because nobody has done anything about them. Examples are: massive lay-offs (mentioned under the heading of 'Too little social embedding'); being passed over repeatedly for promotion; loss of rights and privileges; loss of certain work outcomes; promises that have not been kept; other injustices; other offences and humiliations. Apart from the fact that these memories in themselves negatively influence the effective functioning of a work situation, it also means that we hardly experience pleasant things as such anymore. Moreover, it means that we tend to approach innovations with suspicion and scepticism, and they may evoke a feeling of acute insecurity.

Conflicts

We mention conflicts here separately because of their own dynamics and their apparent inevitability in spite of everyone's good intentions (van de Vliert, 1996). Conflicts stem from the incompatibility of the goals and approaches of different employees, teams, or departments. One party cannot proceed with their plans without resistance from another party, because the other party, often quite justifiably, experiences the activity as an intrusion on their own interests. Often, conflicts are characterized by the prolonged experience of strong emotions such as anger or bitterness, which demand everyone's attention at the expense of attention to the work itself. When a conflict takes a more covert form – open anger is usually frowned upon – it can exist for a very long time as a so-called 'cold conflict'. In such a case, we have to consider everyone's feelings and when we do touch a sensitive spot things can flare up again immediately. It also makes everybody's work more complicated, especially when each party experiences all activities of the other party as intrusions. An annoying characteristic of conflicts is that they tend to become more intense, without anyone actually benefiting.

Conflicts can arise in different ways. Some stem from a 'built-in' antithesis between individual jobs, teams, or departments: the realization of one party's goals interferes with the other party's goals, with all the distorted perception that goes with it. Conflicts can also stem from experiencing stress, which can lower the thresholds for impatience, irritation, and hostility considerably. Sometimes a personal factor plays a part: some people are more inclined to conflict than others.

Uncertainty about the future of one's job and organization

As a consequence of the increased changeability of organizational environments, there is more uncertainty about the stability of organizations and jobs. Also, this changeability leads to large-scale changes in the jobs themselves. The goals that we seek to achieve become more relative in nature, losing a great element of their structuring and motivating effects. Pursuing these goals in work then loses some of its meaning, so the work can less easily hold our attention. Also, in such circumstances, we are haunted by all kinds of unpleasant future scenarios, which cause us anxiety and disquiet, and hamper task performance further. If we are also responsible for the fate of other people, inside or outside of the organization, it can make things worse.

An important point in this respect is that it becomes gradually less likely that we shall work for the same organization for our whole life. This has resulted in a growing emphasis on lifetime 'employability', the ability to keep ourselves employable in a meaningful way, meeting our own purposes and goals in life. In the present state of labour market relations, this tendency raises serious difficulties for those groups of employees in the older age brackets. Though the logic behind it still raises many questions (training employees for the benefit of the competition, the effects on employees' loyalty), this development also implies more positive aspects such as more self-direction, more possibilities for development, and more freedom for employees.

Continual discourteous treatment

Though we might have dealt with continual discourteous treatment under the heading of 'Too much social embedding', we include it here because, in the long run, when we find ourselves experiencing this on an ongoing basis this can primarily affect our own perceived security. Some occupations are structured in such a way that their staff encounter many dissatisfied people, who take out their dissatisfaction on the employees in question, thus having a negative impact on their ability to function effectively. Examples are the jobs of police officer, bailiff, tax officer, social security official, shop assistant, cashier, and bus driver.

Self-Assessment Questionnaire – 13

Too Little Safety Checklist

Place a cross (X) in the 'Yes' column for each form of too little safety that is a source of stress for you.

Forms of too little safety	Yes
Hold-ups, accidents, and client aggression	—
Having witnessed massive lay-offs in your own department	—
Intimidation	—
Sexual harassment	—
Serving as a scapegoat	—
Malicious or unreliable colleagues and bosses	—
Open conflicts	—
Being passed over for promotion	—
Loss of rights and privileges	—
Broken promises	—
Unjust treatment	—
Being offended and humiliated	—
Uncertainty about the future of one's job	—
Uncertainty about the future of one's organization	—

Too much safety

Too much safety is not good either. Paying disproportionate attention to procedures that result in more security may interfere with the ability to function effectively in our real work. Also, a completely safe environment works like a sedative. It makes us lazy and self-satisfied: we think that we have it made and forget that though this situation may be very secure, it may not last for our whole working life. Such an environment diminishes the necessity of using our initiative, taking responsibility, and developing our careers. This leads to too much and too meticulous repetition which, in the long run, makes it hard to keep our attention on our work and so may lead to stress again. In addition, there is the danger of decreasing flexibility and employability. We become so specialized that a lateral move does not seem feasible anymore, while we cannot climb any higher in the organizational hierarchy than the highest level of our own department (which we may have reached a long time ago already). In short, we get trapped in our own job.

In the following sections we will describe a number of variants of these ceiling effects, with the common characteristic that we do not dare to give up our job security. Often, several of these effects are at work at the same time. Lastly, we examine a kind of organizational culture that underlies four of these five ceiling effects.

Experience concentration

In general, we tend to seek out too much safety for ourselves. We want to be good at something. That is why we invest in skill development and learn how to perform in a limited area: we specialize. That gives us a stable repertoire of successful behaviour, appropriate thoughts and feelings. However, the problem is that we develop ourselves solely within the narrow limits of our job: we learn more and more about less and less. We become super-experts who can no longer be deployed elsewhere, a process called 'experience concentration'. This can lead to stagnation, makes our job less engaging, and may lead to a form of qualitative task underload. Its effects become especially damaging when the organization changes so that our job disappears. Essentially, this is also a consequence of failing career policies that do not pay sufficient attention to horizontal mobility, further training, and education. Several Dutch studies show that this occurs quite frequently, particularly among employees over 40.

The 'golden cage' syndrome

Another factor that contributes to too much safety is a good salary. When we earn a high income, it is often impossible to make the same amount of money elsewhere. This can cause us to remain in a position that does not really challenge us any more when it comes to work content, which makes it less easy to keep our mind on our work.

The Peter Principle

A still more vicious scenario is that of being continually promoted as long as we do well in our successive jobs, but eventually getting stuck in a job that we are not competent at. After that, the golden cage syndrome takes over. The general idea is that in the long run incompetent people will occupy all key positions in the organization. Though, of course, organizations exist where this principle has played a part (e.g. bureaucracies where effectiveness is less important), this principle is probably not wholly realistic, being based on out-of-date propositions. It sees careers as being strictly vertical, a job as something unchangeable that cannot be adapted to our needs, and success as the sole determinant of promotion. Lastly, it ignores the possibility of appointing a competent assistant who can do the things that we can't do. Nevertheless, certainly within bureaucracies, such a mechanism can lead, in individual cases. to ceiling effects that can be very unpleasant for all involved.

Being kicked upstairs
Sometimes, bureaucracies solve problems of incompetent or unpopular officials by promoting them to higher but essentially unimportant positions, because they cannot do much harm there. There is no obvious loss of face – after all, they are promoted and get a higher salary – and they do not bother others anymore. However, everybody involved knows that they have been sidetracked. Though such a position offers, in principle, great opportunities to those who enjoy freedom and like to design their own job, such a position can often lead to stress-related reactions and complaints.

The glass-ceiling effect
The glass ceiling effect refers to the phenomenon that it is nearly impossible for certain groups of employees (women, employees of cultural minorities, religious, racial, or ethnic background) to rise above a certain level in the organization, although this is not made clear to them when they join the organization. The word 'glass' refers to the fact that the ceiling is invisible: the unreachable levels are clearly visible and seem easily reachable. This effect stems from deeply rooted premises about the nature of reality (and, for this reason, could have been dealt with under the heading 'too little compatibility of values and goals'), namely the suppositions underlying the division of power and roles.

   People who are troubled by the glass ceiling often have the capacities as well as the ambition to work at a higher lever. At school and in the organization itself, they were told that everybody has the same chances: it's just a matter of working hard and performing well. So, they work hard and perform well, to later discover that this does not play such an important part as was suggested by others. At the same time, they witness colleagues and subordinates who come from the right group progressing in their careers. As a result, many of these employees become frustrated and cynical, and show all kinds of burn-out symptoms.

Too 'secure' an organizational culture

The first four ceiling effects mentioned above – the glass ceiling is different – occur mainly in organizational cultures where older people enjoy a protected status and a friendly climate has become the norm. In such a culture, people do not hold each other responsible for their performances and failures. Moreover, there is often a taboo on every perceptible form of mutual competition. Such a work environment may be very disheartening to some people: it makes no difference what we do or don't do. This can make it hard to keep our mind on the work and to perform well, particularly when others perceive good performance as threatening and see it as showing off.

Self-Assessment Questionnaire – 14

Too Much Safety Checklist

Place a cross (X) in the 'Yes' column for each form of too much safety that is a source of stress for you.

Forms of too much safety	*Yes*
Attention to safety procedures at the expense of attention to the real work	—
Overspecialization	
Lack of work experience outside the present job	—
The feeling of being trapped in a job	—
Having been side-tracked	—
Having been 'kicked upstairs'	—
Staying in a job only because one would earn less money elsewhere	—
Being friendly and a good atmosphere as a norm	—
Enjoying a protected position	—
No appeal to one's responsibilities	—
No appeal to one's performance	—
Absence of all kinds of mutual competition	—
Belonging to the wrong group when it comes to being promoted	—

Too little compatibility of values and goals

Performing a task within an organization that uses methods or sets goals that we find senseless or despicable can make our own performance senseless or despicable as well, even if the task in itself does not evoke problems. Most of the time, this is not an important issue, because such compatibility happens more or less by itself (Schneider, 1987; see 2.2). But though vegetarian butchers and teetotal innkeepers are rare, not everybody has complete freedom of choice in choosing an occupation. Also, the quality of an organization's selection procedure may be improved upon or the result of a choice can be disappointing.

Problems arise mainly when an organization changes and resets the priority of certain goals and values (in the case of a reorganization, merger, privatization, or a new manager). Goals such as quantity of production, flexibility, and being market-directed can become more prominent, while values such as technical perfection and professional freedom can lose their dominant role. However, the latter values may well have been the very reason we wanted to work for the organization in question. The organizational changes then leave us with work that has been stripped of a great part of its challenge and meaning. Though it is easy to describe such a development in terms of personal motivational problems and to deal with it accordingly, it is important to realize that its causes lie in the cultural change. Because changes are especially far-reaching for people who have worked for a long time in a certain way, here we pay particular attention to issues that are important for older employees.

Content of changes

The most important problem with many cultural changes, especially for employees over 50, is that many of these changes go against what our organizations used to expect of us. During our working life, many of us have effectively unlearned to act in the way that the organization now demands as the norm. Organizations now have to become flatter, as well as more flexible, transparent, less product-oriented and more market-oriented, and so on. The principal consequence is that we have to become more autonomous, decisive, and creative: we have to act as if we were 'internal entrepreneurs', who work for ourselves and not for an organization owned by other people. Some of us experience problems with that: the formula 'be free and serve us: make us rich' strikes them as absurd. Moreover, older employees have often learned – mostly the hard way – to mistrust management intentions. Talk about employability and the disappearance of lifetime employment, for example, are not particularly reassuring to them. With older employees, this can evoke strong resistance against these innovations, which can hamper their implementation and make it more likely that they will trigger stress-related complaints.

The changing perspective of ageing employees

The changing perspective of ageing employees is another mechanism that threatens their person–environment fit. Their goals in work change, and this can interfere with the organization's interests as perceived by their superiors, and thus can cause stress. Employees over 50, compared with their younger colleagues, are usually less focused on enlarging their income. They know that it is improbable that their income will increase substantially. They have developed their own lifestyle, attuned to their income, and are not strongly motivated on this point. They have come to realize that they have a finite amount of time and focus more on the here and now, and focus on conserving what they have. That is why they do not like radical reorganizations and the adaptations that those demand from them. In addition, they have gone through a lot of reorganizations already and have little cause to be impressed by the quality of their implementation and results.

The generation gap

Employees belong to different generations, each characterized by its own value orientation, which means that they look at reality in different ways. The value orientations and points of view of the different generations are not always compatible. The so-called 'baby boom' generation (born between 1945 and 1960), for example, usually think differently about many issues from the generations before and after them (Schabracq & Winnubst, 1996a, 1996b). These differences can cause conflict between generations and can give rise to mutual prejudice and stereotypes. In this way, problems can arise which may lead to stress.

Self-Assessment Questionnaire – 15

Too Little Compatibility of Values and Goals Checklist

Place a cross (X) in the 'Yes' column for each form of too little compatibility of values and goals that is a source of stress for you.

Forms of too little compatibility of values and goals	Yes
Resistance against:	
the disappearance of craftsmanship	____
the disappearance of the importance of technical perfection	____
having to be more autonomous, decisive, and creative	____
training	____
having to be employable	____
reorganizations	____
job changes	____
job redesign and changes in tasks	____
the values of the older generation	____
the values of the younger generation	____
violations of the rules	____
political games	____
not being recognized for what you are worth	____
rules that are more important than people	____
being thwarted in your objectives	____
work that does not allow for competition	____
not being allowed to come up with new and creative solutions	____
work that is too much a matter of routine	____
work that does not allow for reflection, overseeing, and understanding	____
having to meet all kinds of requests from all kinds of people	____
work that has too few practical implications	____
working for people who cannot be trusted	____
work that is not up to the state of the art	____
work that does not allow for any personal freedom	____
intrusions on your position and your department	____
intrusions on your ways of working	____
the way your executive operates	____
ways of working that go against your ideas about how people should relate to each other	____
other value changes	____
other changes in goals	____

Too much compatibility of values and goals

Giving more than we get

When we embrace organizational values and goals so intensely that we cannot keep our distance and say no to what we see as our calling, we keep taking more and more on. Because in this way we bite off more than we can chew, this becomes a source of stress and can result in burnout and sometimes ME. In practice, this boils down to the mirror image of stardom, which we dealt with under the heading 'Unbalanced social exchange, getting more than we give'. Here, it is about unbalanced social exchange where we give more than we get. Examples are to be found in the care-giving professions and the social sector, which indicates that this is also a matter of the organizational culture. Too big a discrepancy, giving much more than we get, counts as an important factor behind burnout (Schaufeli & Buunk, 1996). Younger people, who have not yet learned to develop and guard their own limits, are often more susceptible to this than older people. The impersonal, sometimes even antisocial, demeanour characterizing burnout (besides exhaustion and performance deterioration) is primarily an awkward form of self-protection.

Self-Assessment Questionnaire – 16

Too Much Compatibility of Values and Goals Checklist

Place a cross (X) in the 'Yes' column for each form of too much compatibility of values and goals that is a source of stress for you.

Form of too much compatibility of values and goals	Yes
Working too hard based on:	
having no clear limits when it comes to work overload	___
finding it unacceptable to say no to requests to do something	___
a deeply felt obligation to accomplish a certain goal	___
a moral obligation	___
seeing the work as intrinsically good	___
feeling obliged to meet the highest standards	___
the idea that other people are much worse off	___
striving for perfection	___
getting recognition	___
wanting to be a model performer	___
wanting to compete and win	___

wanting to be absolutely original —
wanting to know and understand it all —
not trusting anyone else sufficiently to delegate tasks to them —
being too eager to engage in new options and tasks —
proving that one can take on anything —
doing all kinds of work for everybody —
believing one would be a less than ideal person if one
    worked less hard —

Imbalance between work and other life realms

We discuss the imbalance between work and other life realms in one subsection, because both forms of imbalance influence and often reinforce each other.

We start with causes of imbalance in the other realms of our lives. Then we go on to discuss the effects of decreasing yields from these other realms on the work that we do. Lastly, we present the possible effects on our out-of-work lives and the work domain itself of work that becomes too fascinating and demanding of our time.Though all of this is inextricably interlinked, we shall try to describe the causal factors separately.

Life events in other life realms
Far-reaching events, 'life events' in a positive or negative sense (see 2.1), in life domains other than work can demand a fundamental adaptation of our life, which demands almost all our attention at once. This makes it impossible to keep our attention on our work. In a positive sense, this can occur when we win a huge amount of money in a lottery or fall obsessively in love (actually, some people work better when they are in love, but again, people differ). In a negative sense, this happens when we are confronted by great losses or problems (an accident, fire, illness, crime, loss of a loved one, a bad marriage, divorce, etc.) that absorb all our attention (and again, some people just retreat into their work then). Traumatic events from the past can still have these effects too. Because we usually have to do our work anyway, the decreased ability to perform our work effectively can cause further stress-related complaints.

Double task load
Less dramatic, but more ongoing demands can have a similar consequence. The role complexity and conflict facing many female –

and some male – employees, who have other demands placed on them from household tasks, raising children, and taking care of handicapped or ill parents, other relatives, or neighbours, can decrease the attention available for work. This 'double' task load can interfere with the effective functioning of the work environment, and can lead to stress-related symptoms.

Decreasing outcomes from the other life realms
At the same time the outcomes of the other life realms decrease. Here, we can think for example of:

- love, personal attention and being emotionally embedded; care (shopping, meals, washing, cleaning, etc.); sports, amusement, rest and recuperation; the outcomes of all kinds of other social and public contacts; general knowledge; sense making. The decrease in these outcomes, and the associated benefits, hampers work effectiveness and can also lead to an individual suffering from stress.

Insufficient attention to other realms
Our work can absorb us too much, at the expense of these other aspects of our lives. This can be a matter of attention only, for example, because problems occur at work which we cannot set aside, but also of both attention and time, such as in the case of overwork and business trips. Apart from the fact that this can lead to a depletion in the possible beneficial outcomes from these other life realms (as described above), with its accompanying effects on the work domain, it can also give subsequent rise to unpleasant events in our non-work life, such as conflict and divorce. Such events then detract from the attention available for the work at hand, and so on. A fairly common course of events is that in reaction to such a crisis we throw ourselves into our work with still more zeal, in order not to face our other problems.

In practice, it is often the case that we cannot pinpoint where problems have started, at work or elsewhere. When our managers do this for us, attributing the disturbed imbalance exclusively to causes in our private life, they do not serve us well. The same occurs when a manager attributes stress or health complaints one-sidedly to our personal weaknesses. Of course, our weak spots break down first when we place ourselves under too much strain, but that is only part of the story. There are also high demands made on us.

By placing responsibility for problems so emphatically outside the organization, the manager does not serve the organization well either. First, it becomes impossible for the organization to improve things. Instead, it puts its fate in the hands of the occupational health services which, paradoxically enough, organizations often do not hold in high esteem. The organization also rejects the option of detecting the underlying causes in the organizational practices by a thorough analysis of the complaints. Although these are probably not the only causes of stress and health complaints and causes of sick leave, it is very likely that they result in more undesirable effects in the organization than stress alone. Here again the story of the mine canary from 2.1 applies.

Of course, the border between work and private life is an issue here. To what degree is the organization allowed to interfere with its employees' private life? Mutual consultation is the logical way to go, here as well as with every intervention. So the organization can offer personal guidance and can ask whether the manager is allowed to bring up certain problems in discussions of progress or at work conferences.

Self-Assessment Questionnaire – 17

Spillover Checklist

Place a cross (X) in the 'Yes' column for each form of too much spillover that is a source of stress for you.

Forms of spillover from private life to work stemming from:	Yes
too many household tasks	——
raising children	——
a handicapped or sick partner	——
handicapped or sick children	——
other problems at home	——
taking care of handicapped or sick parents, other relatives or neighbours	——
other paid work	——
unpaid work	——
hobbies	——

Forms of spillover from work to private life, resulting in too little time and attention for:	
your partner	——
your children	——

your relatives	——
your friends	——
other social and public contacts	——
your own household tasks	——
sports	——
leisure and cultural activities and amusement	——
rest and recuperation	——
holidays	——
developing your general knowledge	——
sense-making	——

Tasks that imply too much challenge

Many people go on working much too hard for much too long. Apart from the fact that this may be reduced to manic power fantasies ('I can take on every challenge') or a masochistic streak ('I can take everything. Nothing really affects me'; see also 2.1 and 2.4), its most obvious outcome is that we do not have to think of anything else. Our work protects us from all possible feelings of dissatisfaction. We don't need to ask ourselves whether this is the life we had imagined, whether our partner is the one with whom we want to grow old, and why and for whom we work so ridiculously hard. In this sense, this is really linked to the previous section on imbalance between work and other life realms.

Work can also contain a level of challenge which is too far beyond our competence. Either everything happens too quickly and we cannot keep up with it, or the task gradually becomes too complicated for us and demands more knowledge, skills, and abilities than we can mobilize. We start to make mistakes. We are no longer able to deal with the task in a systematic way, or survey things properly. We experience mental chaos and task performance breaks down. When we still have to perform our task, this can become a major source of stress. The following issues can also play a part:

Too many things to do in too little time
Doing many things at high speed can be very pleasant, especially when everything goes well. Deadlines can be pleasant challenges. We can surprise ourselves, be proud of our performance, and enjoy relaxing afterwards – when everything goes well. It becomes a different story when things are not going well; for example when we:

are not in the mood; are angry about the way in which our manager allocated us this work; are tired; cannot keep our mind on our work; feel that we are not really doing very well.

When, on such an occasion, the deadline is difficult to meet, it becomes harder to work ourselves up to it. Deadlines should not be too hard and too many. However, the concept of 'just in time' management has increased the number of hard deadlines in all kinds of work greatly. 'Just in time' management is based on the idea that things should be ready or available just in time, not too late and not too early. This prevents stocks of materials, half-products, and completed products from piling up, getting in the way, and demanding extra storage room while they do not generate any returns.

Tasks that are too difficult

Difficult tasks that we can only just handle have similar effects to the above, in a positive as well as a negative sense.

It's a different scenario when some parts of the work are already too difficult to begin with, due to the fact that we lack the necessary experience or training, for instance in the case of new tasks. We then make a lot of errors and task performance becomes chaotic. Attempts to repair the mistakes take a lot of time, and are not always successful. We can then try to work around the problems and to get some of the work done anyway, if that is at all possible. Things become especially disturbing for us when the tasks that we are finding difficult used to be relatively straightforward. An example is a new word processor or other computer program, which we are not used to, and where commands for all kinds of familiar tasks are almost opposite to those of the former program. This is another example of where the need to do the job regardless of the problems can lead to the experience of stress.

Serious consequences

The challenge presented by a particular task becomes greater in proportion to the degree that the consequences of doing it wrongly become more serious. This occurs for instance when we have to take decisions that have serious consequences for different parties. We are likely to make mistakes, particularly when we do not possess all the necessary information, which is often the case. Still, we do not want others to suffer from this and we want to do everything correctly, which is impossible, and is likely to cause stress. Because of the fact that organizations have become flatter and autonomous task teams are on the rise, people who are used to doing what the boss says now have to take such decisions themselves. For these people, having this level of discretion to take such decisions can create a considerable extra workload.

Too great an appeal to someone's personal motives and talents

When a task coincides too much with what we like and what we are good at, it can become too challenging in the sense that we can become lost in the task to the extent that we do little else. Essentially, this is a variant of the unbalanced social exchange relationship of giving more than we get, though this type usually is of much less concern. Well-known examples are the obsessed romantic artists in their attic, who in spite of hunger, cold, tuberculosis, and other miseries, work only at their art, and their modern counterparts, the grey-faced computer nerds who spend the whole night in front of the screen.

Ambiguities

With many tasks, it is not completely obvious what is expected of us. The challenge then is to do well anyway, to the degree of the perceived expectations. When the ambiguities are too great, or when we take them too seriously, the ability to carry out the task effectively becomes less likely and stress can be the result. Ambiguity can take many forms. Sometimes, the goals of the task are unclear ('I more or less manage things around here.'). Sometimes, it is the way in which the goals have to be attained ('How you do it doesn't interest me much. I don't even want to know, as long as you do it.'). Sometimes too, it is a matter of insufficient feedback ('Did it work out?' 'We'll know more in five years.'). Other issues that can bring about stress complaints are unclear responsibilities ('I think you should take this up with Peterson.' 'No, Johnson, I've got to have you.'); appointments ('I told you it would be soon.'); criteria for performances and quality ('You meant something like this?'); and so on.

Too many divergent responsibilities

When a task brings too many divergent responsibilities, the result may be a decrease in effectiveness. To begin with, such a task demands that we mentally change gear a lot, in respect of both problems and people. It also means that we are doing very different things, have to keep many loose ends in our heads and are never ready, because then the next responsibility emerges. As a result, we cannot really relax and recover. Furthermore, the ways in which we deal with the different responsibilities interfere with each other from time to time, where the timely completion of the one makes the timely completion of the other impossible, and vice versa (a familiar problem for many secretaries).

Incompatible responsibilities

A special case of divergent responsibilities is role conflict, or incompatible responsibilities. A familiar example is the position of the lower or middle manager. When such a person pleases their superior by increasing production, they may evoke a conflict with the department's employees. This is not only a matter of the employees not wanting to work harder, but also because they want to see their manager as the advocate of their interests. However, when our poor lower or middle manager enthusiastically takes on such a role, they risk a conflict with the management. The dilemma is obvious: what is good in the eyes of one party is wrong in the other's, and vice versa. Though a completely perfect and correct task performance, to the full satisfaction of both parties, will always be problematic, the manager in question has still been hired to do as good a job as he or she can.

Self-Assessment Questionnaire – 18

Too Much Task Challenge Checklist

Place a cross (X) in the 'Yes' column for each instance of too much task challenge that is a source of stress for you.

Instances of too much task challenge	Yes
Working under constant time pressure	___
Short-term deadlines	___
Much overtime	___
Tasks that are too difficult	___
Incompatible responsibilities	___
Incompatible tasks	___
Unclear tasks	___
Unclear targets	___
Insufficient knowledge of work results and outcomes	___
Unclear responsibilities	___
Unclear appointments criteria for performances and quality	___
Too varied work task	___
Too much autonomy	___

Too much work in too little time	___
Too fast work pace	___
Too many deadlines	___
Too divergent responsibilities	___
Too many responsibilities	___

Tasks that imply insufficient challenge

When work does not offer sufficient challenges to hold our attention but we still have to perform the task, we have to switch over to another kind of attention: we have to force ourselves to keep our mind on our work. Such a forced form of attention soon becomes very tiring. We can only go on in such a way for a limited period of time. Attention is diverted, we become strangely sleepy, we have to yawn, and it becomes more and more difficult to deal with the task. This makes us less effective in our work, and can evoke stress.

When nothing or almost nothing has to be done, it is often difficult to do something else. This is also a matter of implicit group pressure: we make corny jokes, try to make each other laugh, and don't work. However, we are not completely free either and five such days in a row are nobody's favourite way of spending time. When the resentment becomes too strong, this actually presents an excellent opportunity to scrutinize the way the organization functions and to look for systemic errors to be corrected. We now look at a number of work situations, which may present insufficient challenge.

Too few activities to fill the time
For many people, having insufficient activities to fill the time in a work situation, while not being allowed to leave either, is intensely unpleasant. This is the stuff that imprisonment is made of. The same goes for too slow a work pace. Eventually, we become drowsy, we get bored, and have difficulty concentrating on the little work we have to do. We become less effective and the chances are that we are going to make more mistakes. Social contacts often play a crucial part here in keeping us alert and focused.

Lack of engagement or a noncommittal attitude
Older employees often find themselves, or steer themselves into, situations where no one expects much of them, and reflect that in their own attitude. Managers often do not appeal to older employees'

responsibilities, even when their performance becomes less than acceptable. This happens especially when the employees are considerably older than their managers. The due respect for these employees, who have won their spurs in the organization a long time ago, often makes it hard for a manager to treat these employees in the same way as they treat younger employees. Correcting these employees may evoke feelings of uneasiness and guilt. Some managers tend to avoid this, with all the expected consequences.

Work with insufficient meaning

Tasks without much meaning appeal insufficiently to our talents and motivations. The effect is that it is hard to keep our attention on the tasks' execution, making these possible sources of stress. Insufficient meaning can have different causes. Some tasks have very little variation and consist of infinitely repeating short episodes. Examples are assembly tasks at a conveyor belt (such as assembling one simple, tiny part), working at a counter selling tickets, or at a call centre. Actually, in the last two examples, the personal contact involved may still appeal to us, certainly at the beginning of a working day. Often such tasks are quite easy, which is not good for concentration either. The lack of meaning can also stem from the remoteness of the task's contribution to the final product ('so I see to it that these little things here are in the correct position when they enter the machine over there').

There are often ways for us to give more meaning to the work. For example, we can treat the work as a ritual or give ourselves additional instructions ('It's an unlucky day for people with green eyes and a blue sweater, they all have to wait for ten seconds'). We can also introduce a game element (e.g. 'The next ten clients I'll do within five minutes, and at least five of them will leave laughing'). Lastly, we can redefine the work, and make it sound nicer ('No sir, I don't wash windows here, I provide you with clear vision'). However, this solution may soon wear thin.

Too little decision latitude

Some tasks are so regulated that there is no freedom to influence the course of affairs in any way ourselves. Everything – breaks, the sequence of tasks, work pace, and so on – is fixed. This occurs for example at counters or call centres, as well as when our work links us up to a machine or assembly line that we cannot influence. In addition, such work is often strictly supervised, with or without the help of electronic devices. So there are cash registers that produce receipts that show not only the goods paid for, the prices, and the final sum, but also the number of seconds that the cashier has taken. Together with the date, the time of day, and the cashier's number, this small slip of paper is turned into evidence about the cashier's performance. Lastly, strict supervision interferes with possibilities for social contacts while working. Because this mostly concerns tasks that also fit under the heading 'work with insufficient meaning', it becomes obvious that this kind of work, when things do not go well, can generate a lot of stress. In order to make our work more pleasant, there remains little but daydreaming or thinking about something pleasant or useful.

Tasks that contain insufficient challenge and tasks with little meaning and decision latitude often have to be done in large quantities and at a fast pace. As a consequence, these tasks also imply too much challenge. Having to do much meaningless work is known as a 'high strain' condition (Karasek and Theorell, 1990). This combination of quantitative overload and qualitative underload has harmful effects on our health and may even contribute to an early death.

Self-Assessment Questionnaire – 19

Too Little Task Challenge Checklist

Place a cross (X) in the 'Yes' column for each instance of too little task challenge that is a source of stress for you.

Instances of too little task challenge	Yes
Too few activities to fill the time	——
Tasks that consist only of being vigilant to something that is not allowed to happen	——
Tasks that are too easy	——
Meaningless tasks	
Irrelevant tasks	
Too little task autonomy	——
Too strict supervision	
Too many instructions	——
Work that demands less knowledge and skill than it used to	——
Too much repetition	——
Too little variation in tasks	——

To take stock of the imbalance between your work and other life realms, you can begin by referring to the Life Events Scale, page 17–18.

4. The approach

4.1 INTRODUCTION

A plan in seven steps

What does a stress management project look like? By focusing attention on the different stages of a project, this chapter provides a plan in seven successive steps. It provides guidelines for project team members, external consultants, and project leaders, given from the perspective of an external consultant. We describe the first steps in most detail, because the problem definition and project design are the most difficult part of the project and demand the greatest effort and creativity from consultants and team members. Elements that play a role in the different steps are outlined in the description of the first step for which they are relevant. The questions and exercises interspersed throughout the text will help you to focus on important issues in the change process. Though these are primarily meant to clarify your own perspective on the related issues, you can also use them to explore the perspectives of the other stakeholders by answering the questions from their point of view.

Time scale

The time scale of a stress management project varies according to the size of the organization, the interventions chosen, and the available personnel. The organizational ability to decide quickly and mobilize the necessary resources and personnel are also important. An average project may take about a year, but we must be able to complete the research and feedback of results within three months. Such a long time scale demands a high level of motivation from all parties involved to keep the project's purpose and results alive. This is why perpetual good communication about the project is crucial.

Warning

The external consultant and team members should accept the fact that stress management projects usually occur in circumstances that are not generally optimal for interventions *per se* in organizations. After all, the organizations involved have failed to examine their own functioning adequately, have resisted changes, or had trouble adapting to them. It is often necessary to investigate their history to find out how the present state has come about. Here, we may be faced with the so-called 'unspeakables' – painful events, differences of opinion and conflicts, which members of the organization don't usually talk about with outsiders (not even with those outsiders who might solve these problems for them, see section 2.2). In order for the project to progress, we usually have to discuss these unspeakables, which is an extremely delicate process that demands courage and faith from all parties.

Your own personal position and attitude

Point for Reflection
As a consultant in a stress management project, it is important to fathom in advance one's own attitude toward stress and its consequences. Before looking at the different project steps, we ask you to focus on these issues with the following questions:

What are your own views on work stress?

What are your reasons for taking on this project?

What consequences may these have for your attitude?

As a result, which aspects of the project will need special attention?

What are your own stress reactions? (see the checklists in section 3.1)

Your most characteristic stress reaction is often an exaggeration of your own most basic positive trait or core motive. Following Daniel Ofman (1995) we call this stepping into your most basic personal pitfall. For instance, an exaggeration of reliability and consistency may become rigidity, while too much carefulness may become suspicion. Finding out about your personal pitfall and core motive can simply consist of asking your 'significant others' (partner, children, best friends) which of your characteristics and habits is the most irritating to them. By asking yourself: 'what inherently positive trait am I exaggerating when I display this characteristic', you may discover your most basic core motive.

In addition, you could ask yourself what kinds of behaviour and what kinds of people irritate you the most. Chances are that these behaviours and people represent the opposite of your own core motive. Ofman (1995) calls this your 'personal allergy'. So if your core motive consists of making things workable, you may be 'allergic' to people who start things up only to disappear when some serious work is needed.

Point for Reflection
Which of your habits and characteristics are the most irritating to your 'significant others'?

How do these habits relate to your habitual stress responses?

If you think of your habitual stress responses as your personal pitfalls, what basically good trait or core motive might you be exaggerating?

What positive impact might this trait have on your contributions to this project?

What negative impact might stepping into your pitfall have on your contributions?

What are your own characteristic sources of stress? (See the checklists in section 3.2)

What kind of people evokes stress in you or irritate you (or to what kind of people are you 'allergic')?

To what degree can they be characterized by traits that are the opposite of your basically good and positive trait mentioned above?

What consequences may this have for your own contributions to the project?

What does this teach you?

4.2 STEP 1: ORGANIZATION AND CONSULTANT FORM A RELATIONSHIP

Occasions and causes

Step 1 starts when the people in charge in the organization realize that stress and its consequences have become a problem: things could be better and something should happen. This understanding can have divergent causes. Examples are problems with a certain area of production, high sick leave, high turnover, or alarming results of a regular health examination. The initiative to articulate the problems in the organization can come from different parties. Line management, human resources, works council, and occupational health services can each play a part here. The first initiative in starting a stress management project can consist, for example, of a management note, or by inviting an expert speaker. When the organization establishes an advice relationship with an occupational health consultant the stress management project has started.

The parties involved

The following parties may play a role in a stress management project:

The employees. The employees have to know and indicate their own limits. In the first instance, they must try to solve their own problems. They can also indicate what stress sources they are encountering in discussions of process or occupational health consultations. For different reasons, such as the characteristics of the organizational culture or their own norms, employees often fail to use these options and, as a result, some employees carry on for too long in spite of complaints, without any adaptations in their work. This occurs especially with older employees with high work standards.

The employer. The employer is legally obliged to supervise work conditions in a way that is tailored to the specific organization. The physical aspects of the work situation are usually given more attention than aspects related to well-being, which are often harder to specify. A policy that also specifies goals for well-being can be an important instrument for initiating stress management.

The manager. Managers play an important part in stress prevention. They do so by signalling and discussing stress complaints, as well as by creating the right conditions for good performance. The latter is a matter of providing employees with sufficient space, information, and attention, and if necessary acting as a coach. Proper feedback in regular talks about the employees' functioning is also important. Here, they can discuss stress reactions and sources, talk about possibilities, and think about solutions. Some training may be of help here (see also the Addendum, section 7). Managers can also call upon the human resources department or consult colleagues, their own manager, or an occupational health service professional. The stress management project's success depends to a large part on the managers' motivation and competence.

The human resources manager. Usually, human resources managers prepare personnel policies and play an advisory role. They can provide important reasons for starting a stress management project based on their education and knowledge about personnel and sick leave data. Also, they can put stress on the agenda by way of their training policy. Human resources managers are also important when it comes to the further careers of individual employees, and often act as intermediaries to external experts such as consultants and trainers.

The occupational health co-ordinator. In a growing number of organizations, an occupational health co-ordinator advises the management on safety, health, and well-being risks. This employee provides information and helps to formulate the occupational health policy, and so can play an important role when it comes to stress management policies.

The occupational health consultant. The occupational health consultant is not directly employed by the organization, but is attached to an occupational health service. There, he or she is usually the proper professional for developing occupational stress management projects. The consultant is able to select, use, and interpret stress research instruments, knows about the various intervention programmes, and helps organizations to implement policies to prevent work stress. An occupational health consultant often serves as the external consultant who helps to start up the stress management project.

The occupational health physician. The occupational health physician may be employed by the organization itself or by an occupational health service. The physician tries to translate individual stress complaints into organizational factors, and co-ordinates various data from their medical consultations, the social-medical team meetings, and research studies. Examples of these data are the results of risk analyses, visits to the work site, and regular occupational health surveys. The physician points out problems to the organization, calls upon other experts to offer the organization tailor-made interventions, and remains involved with the follow-up of stress management projects.

The company welfare worker. Some organizations employ company welfare workers, who are knowledgeable about stress as well as about the organization in question, where they often have access to key people. They can play an important part in a stress management project, particularly with the problem definition, the choice of an advisory committee, and the interventions' implementation. Moreover, the company welfare worker can provide individual care such as therapy and coaching, and can refer to other professionals.

The employees' representatives. The works council or a possible occupational health committee can contribute to improvements in working conditions. They can advise about project design and increasing support on the shop floor, as well as about implementation of interventions.

Care systems outside of the organization. A stress management project can also use or refer to care systems outside of the organization. For example, employees can be referred to experts such as general practitioners, psychotherapists, welfare workers, and lawyers. If necessary, a visit from the health and safety authorities can also be requested.

Point for Reflection
With whom do you have to relate in the project (team members, representatives of all parties, etc.)? Make a list of names. Imagine each of them in your mind's eye and for each of them try to answer the following questions.

When you picture X, what kind of mood do they display?

What kind of associations does X evoke in you?

What do you like about X?

What do you dislike about X?

How does this relate to your answers to the previous questions about your own stress reactions and sources?

What does this teach you?

Try to take X's perspective.

How would X see you from their position, with their interests?

What would X want from you, and what would X not want from you?

How might you reward or punish X?

Characteristics

By contrasting the desired future situation with the undesired present situation, we evoke a tension that can serve as a generator to the change project. This step is about projecting a general direction for the solution as well as a global preliminary goal from the status quo. An important talent here is the ability to quickly discern the most relevant constraints and flaws in the existing reality and to feel their impact, as well as to envision a technically ideal situation. The most important differences between the status quo and the ideal situation then point to possible improvements. The steering principle in this stage consists mainly of together attempting a 'perfect' result. The pleasure in this stage comes from starting up a good project together: having a joint vision of how we can make things better.

The consultant or project manager should, as soon as possible, gain a good perspective of the organization, its place in its environment, and the determining factors there. Besides consulting the available documentation and experts, this will mainly arise from the first visits to the organization. The consultant at this stage sniffs the atmosphere, observes how people relate to each other, assesses their mood, and maps what can be noted about stress. In addition, the consultant interviews key players to find out about their points of view, and asks for relevant archive data.

Point for Reflection

When you are becoming engaged with an organization, it is advisable to examine your own attitude and possible prejudices towards the organization in question. You may ask yourself the following questions:

What is your attitude toward the organization and its line of business in general?

What does the organization look like (general style, interior design, furniture, state of repair, and cleanliness)?

How do people dress?

What is their prevalent mood?

What is the atmosphere like: how does it feel and what effects does that have on you?

How may these effects influence your contributions?

Point for Reflection
The consultant has to find out who in the organization sees what as a problem. This implies the following questions:

What do the organizational representatives describe as a problem?

Do they point out culprits?

How valid is the problem they sketch?

Is it solvable in this form?

What hidden agendas might be involved?

During the first step, it is important to get an overall picture of the problem and possible solutions. The consultant also needs to know about the factors underlying the decision to start a stress management project and the wishes of the different organizational parties and levels in this respect. So the consultant has two agendas: a more technical, content-oriented one and a more political-relational one, each with its own issues. Because it is still unclear whether the consultant will be given the contract to conduct a project, and since the consultant's business interests are involved, this can be difficult. After all, the client wants a solution: an approach with a budget, as simple, quick, and cheap as possible, and preferably without overturning things too much. However, persistently asking questions is the best way to get a good idea of the problem and possible solutions.

Nevertheless – and this is very important – you have to remember that you are not only there to find things out at this stage. You are also there to establish relationships. This means that you have to attend as fully as possible to all your interaction partners, not only by listening to their words but also by really being with them: feeling what they feel, thinking what they think, and letting them be aware of this. In behavioural terms this may mean being sufficiently alert, keeping sufficient eye contact, nodding, mirroring facial expressions and tone of voice, and synchronizing speech and movements.

Technical and content-oriented issues

On the technical and content-oriented side of the analysis, the following issues are important during the first meetings with the client and other stakeholders.

The organization in its environment

During the first step, the consultant tries to get a global impression of the organization and its environment. This involves the field the organization is in, its culture, and its health.

To gain a picture of the environment, the consultant seeks information about the following issues:

- environmental conflicts and hostility and the organization's position in market developments:
  - how do supply and demand develop?
  - what does the competition look like?
  - where does the organization stand compared to the competition?
- the new technological developments;
- sociocultural changes;
- developments in the political and legal area.
(For an extensive overview see Gordon, 1991.)

The professional involved may ask the following questions:

- What products and services does the organization deliver and how successful is it in this respect?
- How does the organization score with respect to other organizations in the same branch?
- What specific demands does the environment pose (by its economic, technological, sociocultural and political–legal changes) to the organization?
- What is characteristic about the organizational culture?
- Is there a clear mission?
- How transparent is the organization?

Stress problems

When we have gained some idea about the organization and its environment, we take a first look at the specific stress risks, their causes and history, and the way in which these risks are related to the work itself and the work environment. The consultant tries to get an idea of their influence on individual functioning and the organization itself, as well as of the differences between groups of people in the organization in these respects. This results in a first estimation of the seriousness and direct costs of the effects of the problems, such as: sick leave; replacement; loss of production. In addition, other negative effects may result, such as: internal conflicts; disturbances of communication with suppliers and clients; missed opportunities; quality deterioration of products; turnover; diminished attraction to potential new employees; and undesired publicity.

The consultant investigates former projects in this area and their results. The following questions may be asked:

- What are the undesired effects caused by stress in the organization?
- Which groups of employees (in terms of jobs and departments) are troubled most by the consequences of stress?
- How can this be pinpointed in the sick leave figures?
- Does there seem to be a causal link?
- What five causes of stress do those involved rank as most important?
- Are there common causes?
- What costs can be associated with stress complaints?
- What other negative effects occur?

Possible solutions

During the appraisal of the problems, the consultant also tries to get an idea of the possibilities and limitations with regard to improvements, including those that individuals involved in the organization observe and generate themselves.

This may lead to the following questions:

- How might we do something about it?
- What causes are the easiest to deal with?
- What solutions do the different parties in the organization envisage themselves?
- Has something been done before about the undesired effects, and with what success?

- What objections and impossibilities block changes?
- From what underlying factors do these objections and impossibilities stem?
- What can we do about these underlying factors?
- What forces can the organization make better use of?
- What 'levers' can we use?
- What kind of side effects may these interventions have?

The consultant's role
The consultant serves as researcher, expert, and facilitator during this step. The consultant arranges the clients' contributions, gives an opinion about the data, and sketches the course of possible solutions. This helps the organization to define its own problems, the desired situation, and the approach.

A workshop for the project decision makers
A good way to create clarity and support is organizing a special workshop (see also the next subsection and Addendum 2.1) for the decision makers involved in initiating a stress management project. In such a workshop, we examine the undesired effects of stress, its causes, points of departure for interventions, their possible undesired effects, and possibilities for preventing or neutralizing those effects. This results in a preliminary action plan, a first inventory of possible specific interventions, and a global idea about the way to evaluate the project (criteria to measure the intended progress, a control group, etc.).

Workshops in general
Workshops are meetings of real-life groups aimed at forming an optimal plan to deal with a particular problem. The workshop facilitator does some research in advance to get a picture of what they can expect. This concerns the immediate issue, but it is also important to get an idea of the points of departure, axioms, perspectives, and interests of all players or parties, and the options and risks they perceive ('What would you do about it if you were in charge here?'). This involves interviews with participants and other informants.

Before the actual workshop, the facilitator discusses the specific goal for the workshop with all the key people involved. At the start of the meeting, the facilitator states the agreed goal, though without talking about specific solutions. For example: 'This meeting's objective is to form a plan for dealing with the stress problems in this organization.' The goal now forms a common point of departure for all participants, and serves as an excellent touchstone for the relevance of everything that happens during the workshop. The facilitator – as well as the other participants – can use it to cut off any irrelevant contribution: 'How does this relate to our purpose?'

When the goal is set, the facilitator presents an agenda and indicates what the workshop's intended outcomes are. For example: 'At the end of the meeting, we must have identified and set a goal, we'll have an idea how to do it, and we'll make a division of roles and tasks, as well as planning a time scale.' We can measure the workshop's success by the progress made with the problems. In principle, we can go on repeating workshops until we have formed a workable plan for solving the problems.

A workshop agenda can involve the following issues:

- Stating the specific goal and intended outcomes for the workshop.
- Becoming aware of certain issues: what is the problem? what undesired effects occur? what positions do people hold? on what suppositions are these based?
- Determining the most important causes of undesired effects and how causes and effect are correlated: what caused it and how is everything connected? (A useful rule of thumb is that 20% of all causes are responsible for 80% of all effects, the so-called Pareto principle.)
- Determining points of departure for interventions.
- Determining and elaborating possible interventions: how can we make things more effective and efficient? how could we make it more pleasant and motivating? how might we all learn more from it?
- Determining potential consequences of interventions: what undesired effects might our interventions cause?
- Coming to an agreement about implementing interventions and dividing individual responsibilities, and roles: who does what? when should what be ready?

(For a schematic review of this approach, see Noreen *et al.*, 1995.)

Workshops have one or two facilitators, for example, a member of the project team and/or an external consultant. They safeguard the conduct of the workshop and try to raise the content quality to the highest possible level. They see to it that participants occupy themselves with what matters at a particular moment and do everything necessary to facilitate its progress. A facilitator turns the progress of the process into a discussion issue. For example:

- 'Where do we stand now?'
- 'At what points did we make progress today and what still has to happen?'
- 'What are our main obstacles?'
- 'What can we do about these?'

Facilitators try to probe the participants' creativity as well. To this end, a facilitator asks questions ('How can we do this better?'). Or they may summarize the participants' contributions ('So, you mean that you don't find it a good plan because it doesn't take into account that…?'). The facilitator can also ask the others to be more specific about what they mean ('Could you give us an example?'). Furthermore, the facilitator can use brainstorming techniques or use exercises and role-play to clarify problems and to appeal to the participants' creativity (see section 4.5).

Political/Relational issues

Besides content-orientated issues, relational and political issues make up an important part of the consultant's agenda. This involves matters such as the importance of the problem as perceived by the different parties in the organization, what they want to do about it, the role they have in mind for the external consultant, and what they find are the best possible solutions. This leads to an image of the organizational force field with respect to the problems and possible solutions, and gives a first indication of what support there is in the organization for the project. To this end, the consultant has to clarify a number of issues, without asking questions that are too direct: because of the sensitivity of these subjects some circumspection is called for.

In general, it has to be clear what parties, interests, and differences of opinions are involved with the problems and possible solutions. This leads to the following questions:

- Who sees themselves as problem keepers?
- Who wants to be involved in solving the problems?
- What interests in the status quo and possible solutions do the different parties have?
- What role do the unions play?

A primary issue is that of the position of the contact person or people. What are their interests in the project and what is their agenda? Are they representatives of the management, human resources, welfare work, the occupational health service, or the works council? What support can they mobilize in the organization, and who are their opponents there?

Resistance

Changes in organizational culture tend to evoke all kinds of resistance (see section 2.2) from different parties. Resistance may occur in all steps of a stress management project, especially in step 2.

Resistance of the decision makers

During step 1, it is mainly the resistance at the top of the organization that demands our attention. Resistance at the top against dealing with organization-related stress risks can be explored during the first meeting or in a workshop. This is done by discussing the stress problems and explaining the different elements of our approach in the management workshop mentioned above. The reactions that this evokes, sometimes after some extra probing, clarify which interventions evoke resistance and why that is the case. At the same time, this discussion also reveals who supports the project and for what reasons.

To increase support, we first try to find out what connects the different parties. Using agreed goals and objectives as points of departure, we discuss the differences, the resistance, and their origins. On what suppositions are the differences and resistance based? How can these suppositions be made compatible with the project and with each other?

In this way, we try to find out how we can meet objections and create solutions that satisfy all parties, the 'win–win' solution. To this end, the consultant has to recognize and acknowledge different points of view. Groups of people with divergent interests almost always differ in the ways in which they define a problem. It is important that each of the diverse diagnoses has some recognizable influence on the proposed approach. At the same time, however, the process asks for just one diagnosis or approach. The consultant has to be constantly aware of this dilemma.

On the whole, the issue is whether we can mobilize sufficient support for a stress management project in the organization. An important aspect here is getting a realistic idea about the resources that the organization wants to provide (in terms of budget and available personnel).

Stress as a personal problem

In many organizations, there is some reluctance to acknowledge that problems with work stress may be an organizational problem. Stress is considered to be a personal problem. This applies to the management as well as the employees. Courses for employees focusing on dealing better with stress complaints are perceived as 'losers' classes', with an accordingly high threshold to enrolling. As described in chapters 2 and 3, the victim is blamed for the problems: managers ascribe the causes of employees' problems to their individual inability to meet the work demands. This inability may be attributed, for instance, to their lack of skills or to personal circumstances.

Point for Reflection
How do you yourself behave in this respect?

Management resistance

Resistance to change is based on the idea of an organization as something fixed, in which we cannot easily change something. As described in section 2.2, organizations resist intrusions, and the changes implied by a stress management approach are certainly intrusions. Such changes also imply that previously everything was being handled badly. Managers for whom this is an unacceptable thought may prefer not to change anything: it would only rock the boat and make things worse. Such managers may not perceive reorganizations, mergers, increased competition, and high turnover as sources of stress, but rather as complicating factors, i.e. as reasons to do nothing about stress prevention for the moment.

Employees' resistance

As described in chapter 2, change also evokes resistance among employees. We are used to doing our work in a familiar way. We have invested in it. Our position and interests have been linked to it. Having a change imposed upon us from above means that we have to give up all that. It also implies, again, that apparently we haven't been doing our work properly up till now. Moreover, we know where we stand now, but we don't know what the future will bring. Having to change becomes an intrusion on our interests. Resistance to change is then a self-evident and natural reaction, on an individual as well as collective level.

Point for Reflection
When have you yourself experienced such resistance lately?

Recognition and discussion

In order to deal with resistance, the consultant first has to recognize and respect the resistance. Examples of resistance are denial of the importance of changing something, individualizing problems ('That's just Johnson') or, on the contrary, making them into a collective phenomenon ('That's just the culture here'). If the consultant spots such resistance, they should acknowledge its existence, importance, and legitimacy, and invite the employees involved to explore its motives further with them. Exploring together the background of the resistance can be very productive, as in this way we encounter valid objections to change. Subsequently, the consultant can invite the employees to think about how these objections could be removed, from the perspective of the possible gains that the project may bring. In this way a new reality can come about, which can support the change.

Exploring resistance together may consist of presenting a possible solution to the people involved, after having asked them to mention all their objections immediately and without any reserve. At the same time, the employees involved are asked to think about improvements that might be made: how can it be done better (more effectively and efficiently), more pleasantly, and instructively? In this way, activating resistance energizes problem solving. It is also useful to ask everybody involved to observe and mention everything that goes wrong during and immediately after a change's actual implementation. For an extensive review of how to deal with resistance to change see Ryan and Oestreich (1998).

Working with projects

One of the important tasks in this first step is convincing management that working with a special project team is a proper way to approach stress problems. This means that we have to get approval to install a project team, for which management provides sufficient time and resources. Working with a project team makes sense for several reasons. A project offers a flexible approach in size and priorities, and is reasonably simple to budget and evaluate. It also enables us to assign responsibilities to individual employees from different disciplines and departments.

The project leader

The project leader is somebody from the organization who serves as the contact person for the stress management project, co-ordinates everything, supervises planning and costs, and serves as representative to the management. The project leader has to be somebody with sufficient formal and informal influence in the organization, as well as sufficient time, motivation, and credibility. That is why the leader should come from the management level or at least have sufficient standing there. Lastly, the project leader's tasks, responsibilities, and power should be clearly defined: there has to be a clear understanding about their role, with the management as well as the other team members and the external consultant.

The project team

The project team is responsible for the project's progress. Apart from the fact that the separate team members have to bring sufficient motivation, enthusiasm, and skill to the task, the team has to be given sufficient time, resources, and power, and also has to be trained properly. Regarding the project team's composition, it is important to include the organization's own experts on occupational health and the managers of the departments that the project is focused on. These managers can look after the project's progress and provide the proper resources. Furthermore, it is important to include a representative of the higher management as well as a key person from the work site (preferably a representative of the works council or unions). The external consultant and corporate physician can serve as appointed advisers of the team.

The selection of team members is, however, mainly a matter of their individual abilities.

Here we can ask the following questions:

- What personal interest do they serve by participating in the project team?
- Has a prospective member the necessary social skills and intelligence?
- Is someone actually in a position to participate?
  - to what degree does the project membership imply too heavy a task load,
  - what tasks can put members into difficult situations,
  - do conflicting tasks occur?
- To what degree does working in a project oppose the normal ways of working?

In short the project team has the following tasks: developing the project plan; serving as contact to other parties; planning and control; creating and increasing support in the organization; supervising the implementation and follow-up of agreed measures; supervising the project's evaluation and accounting.

Supervisory committee

During this step, we must also get approval to install a separate supervisory committee. This can advise about translation of research data into practice, the workshops' contents, the feasibility of partial projects, and their contents. The human resources manager and the corporate physician are logical candidates for this committee.

Lastly, it is important to make a preliminary timetable and set dates for meetings.

Pitfalls and learning opportunities

The first step in a stress management project is littered with pitfalls, and the following subsections can be used as a checklist for them. It would be nice if we could avoid all of these, but it is unlikely. However, thinking of Nietzsche's saying that everything that does not kill us will make us stronger, we can reformulate falling into a pitfall as a learning opportunity. This presupposes that we really try to pay attention to these issues and work hard to make the best of them.

Insufficient support from management

The most important pitfall is lack of real involvement and practical support from management. In practice, this usually means that the management provides insufficient resources (finance, people, time) for interventions. A frequently recurring pattern is that management uses a stress management study as a move in a political game with employees and their representatives (works council and unions). The management objective in this case is preserving the status quo. In such a case, management buys research, preferably from a reputed specialized research firm. In this way, they show that they take the stress problems seriously, though without any genuine intention to intervene. Most of the time, the employees' representatives are satisfied: they have got their study and that counts as a victory. The study thus replaces interventions, and so the energy to do something real about the problems is skilfully drained. Then something else comes up that demands everyone's attention, and the research results – which were never meant to be spectacular in the first place – disappear in the organizational archives. The research firm will not tell tales either. They make their living from this kind of assignment and often do not possess the expertise to do anything real about the problems.

One right solution

Another pitfall in this step is the idea of the one right solution. This is closely linked to the rigidity of an expert approach that starts out from a well-described frame of reference. A sociotechnically educated expert, for example, may try to explain everything by task characteristics, while a clinical psychologist may only produce 'psychological' explanations. In this way, both will overlook some causes and suggest inadequate solutions. A related approach is applying methods just because one has them available. In the above example, this almost invariably boils down to either job redesign – preferably in autonomous task teams – or psychotherapy of the kind in which the psychologist at hand has been trained.

Technical pitfalls

There are many kinds of technical pitfalls, including:

- insufficiently reviewing the organization's state and environment and so overlooking the fact that the organization is not in a position to do much about stress, for example, because it is on the verge of being bought or merged;
- focusing exclusively on one or several symptoms such as sick leave or production errors, while not attending to the causal factors;
- ignoring bad experiences with former attempts to do something about stress in the organization;
- ambiguously formulated goal-setting and evaluation criteria.

Political pitfalls

Dealing with the political agenda may lead to the following pitfalls:

- overlooking or marginalizing the interests and resistance of one or more parties in management;
- identifying too much with one party, especially the management;
- becoming too dependent on others for solutions;

- overlooking or marginalizing experts in composing the project team.

Psychological pitfalls

Psychological pitfalls stem from the consultant's emotional peculiarities. Examples include:

- postponing activities too long out of fear of failure;
- throwing oneself into an unknown adventure;
- indignation, accusations, and getting involved in conflicts;
- resistance against working in a project.

Point for Reflection
What are the obvious things you can do in order not to step into these pitfalls? What else might you be able to do in this respect?

Table 4.1: Checklist of outcomes of step 1

Place a cross (X) in the 'Yes' column for each accomplished outcome.

Accomplished outcomes	*Yes*
A decision to start a stress management project	___
Insight into the available resources	___
Insight into the different problem definitions and interests	___
Insight into the political relationships in the organization	___
Sufficient motivation and support for the project	___
A preliminary description of the project's goal setting	___
Some idea about the project's approach and size, costs and gains	___
Some idea about the project's evaluation (see section4.4)	___
The composition of the project team	___
The composition of the advisory committee	___

4.3 STEP 2: GETTING ESTABLISHED

General remarks

In the second step, we elaborate on the layout of the approach together with the other parties involved. The project team and the advisory committee are installed and their tasks have to be clarified. During this step, the most important goal is to create sufficient freedom of action for the project by involving all stakeholders and securing their support and co-operation. This involves active support from the organization as well as guarantees and involvement from the top.

An important talent for you as a project member or consultant in this step is the ability to quickly ascertain someone's position, attitude, wishes, and anxieties: how powerful are they and what do they want? Moreover, it is also important to learn about how you personally would feel about the changes to be made. Again, freedom of action for the team – stemming from sufficient connection with and support from the organization – is the guiding principle here.

The pleasure in this step lies with the opportunities to see and determine together what improvements are possible for all parties involved, leading to broad and solid support for the project. With each possible solution, the key criteria are the extent to which options contribute to production quality, motivation, and job satisfaction, and the personal and professional development of those directly involved.

Activities in step 2

During this step the following activities take place: training the project team; communication about the project; force field analysis and increasing the project's support; research into the organizational culture.

Training the project team
One of the key activities is motivating and training the project team. In the first instance, this is a task for the external consultant, but specialists can be called in for certain aspects. The training consists of the following elements:

- knowledge about the nature, reactions, and sources of stress, tailored to the particular organization (see chapters 2 and 3);
- knowledge about the approach described in this chapter;
- social skills in the areas of interpersonal perception, team roles, team building, motivating, goal setting, interviewing, coaching, brainstorming, dealing with conflicts, conducting workshops, and delegating;
- knowledge about the particular organizational culture;

- knowledge about relevant research methods and instruments, including evaluation research methods and interviewing;
- knowledge about resistance to change, training in dealing with resistance, and creating support;
- developing a project plan, including definitive goal setting;
- knowledge of interventions;
- maintaining contact with all relevant parties, being able to refer, and some insight into power problems.

Point for Reflection
What knowledge and skills would you personally need to acquire in this respect?

Communication about the project
Providing proper information is crucial when introducing a stress management project. Employees have to be stimulated to think about the project and to determine their positions. Another important goal is developing a common conceptual framework. Here, we have the following resources at our disposal: project presentations; corporate publications; presentations by experts, live or on video, and special activities; presentations during work progress meetings.

Project presentations. The goal of project presentations is to elucidate the project's content and importance. The following issues can be reviewed: the immediate cause of the project; the purpose of the project; an abstract of the project's content; relationships between sick leave, stress, and organizational characteristics; the roles of management and works council; consequences of implementing stress management; answering questions and discussing objections. All this can offer a framework for talking and thinking about stress risks and the overall approach.

Corporate publications. Many organizations periodically publish a newsletter or magazine describing developments in the organization. The introduction of a stress management project can be an occasion for a 'special feature' about this subject, including short questionnaires and interviews with the works council, managers, the project leader, and employees from different departments.

Expert presentations and special activities. A presentation by an authority in the area of stress and stress management, a video presentation, and short-term special activities are good ways of launching a discussion about the issue.

Presentations during work progress meetings. Issues that we can deal with here are:

- the reason for the project and some explanation of the concept of work stress;
- a concise and clear review of the project's purpose and content;
- the points of view of management and works council;
- explaining project steps and planning;
- explaining the questionnaire and confidentiality rules;
- introducing project group members who can be called upon to answer questions;
- answering questions arising from the presentation and discussing objections.

Point for Reflection
Which of these ways of communicating would be possible in your case?

Force field analysis

In order to analyse the force field – the stress problems and their solutions – the consultant goes into the organization, together with a team member, to interview the stakeholders (this too is a part of their training). Just as in step 1, the consultant and team members have a double agenda: a technical, content-oriented agenda and a political, relational one. Here, the emphasis is even more on the political, relational one. As Joan Meyer (1994) says, a force field analysis implies that we depart from a preliminary goal definition and try to take stock of the forces we can use to realize the desired purpose, as well as of the forces that, for the moment, hamper goal attainment. This involves reviewing the motives (habits, needs, goals, rewards, objections, and punishments) and limitations of all parties involved relative to the different project stages.

We then try to increase support by finding solutions that overcome the objections and limitations, together with the employees who are directly involved. By challenging those involved to respond to the different aspects of the approach and ask pertinent questions, the nature of the resistance and its premises quickly become clear. We also ask what options for improvement they can envisage (see section 4.2).

We may ask the following questions:

- How do the different parties define stress?
- What stress causes and effects do the different parties mention?
- What possibilities for interventions do the different parties envisage?
- What consequences do the proposed interventions have for the different parties?
- To what degree do these interventions interfere with the normal ways of working?
- How do the proposed interventions relate to the organizational HRM policies?
- What reactions would the project evoke in other departments and how might we deal with that?
- How is it that until now no form of stress management has been developed?
- How can we improve the project's effectiveness at certain points?
- How can the project contribute to greater motivation and more job satisfaction among the employees in question?
- How can the project contribute to employees' development and their employability in and outside the organization?

Research into the organizational culture

It is important for the external consultant to develop an intimate knowledge of the organizational culture. Only then can the consultant relate to the ways of thinking, feeling, and acting which make up everyday reality in the organization. This is different for the project team members, because they are already immersed in this culture. For them, it is more a matter of trying to distance themselves so as to see everyday organizational reality through the eyes of an outsider. The purpose of a culture study is to find out to what extent problems are linked to cultural characteristics, as well as to what extent proposed solutions are compatible with the culture. An important point here is to discuss – first within the team and later outside it – matters that are unthinkable and unspeakable within the organizational culture (see section 2.2). This entails gaining a perspective on organizational history by examining past events that had an influence on the organization (see table 4.2).

Table 4.2: Researching organizational culture

Research methods:
interviews (individual, groups),
observation, using yourself as an instrument,
questionnaires,
studying and analysing archive data.

Research goals:
Making a historical sketch: determining the developmental stage, tracking the consequences of important and traumatic events, such as:
• reorganizations and mergers,
• massive layoffs,
• ethical problems.

Determining the kind of organization with the help of the categories that Charles Handy (1978) describes, namely the organization as:
• bureaucracy, where everything centres around prescriptive rules,
• social club, where personal relations are all-important (who says what, who you know, and how you stand with the important people),
• pragmatic and goal-oriented network, where the focus is on project development and accomplishing objectives in changing teams,
• collection of individual professionals, where experts are each doing their thing.

Detecting:
• typical forms (ways of doing, saying, thinking and feeling, dress code, style, interior decor, architecture),
• mythology (stories about organizational heroes and villains),
• norms (the dos and don'ts underlying the forms, resulting in everyday conduct and its blind spots),
• values and axioms underlying reality.

Tracing and determining problems.
Determining consequences for solutions.

Kinds of problem:
• bottlenecks and stress sources,
• blind spots:
• unspeakables,
• unthinkables,
• collective defence mechanisms,
• stereotyping and prejudices (sex, age, profession, former organization, cultural and ethnic background).

Preventing and dealing with:
• sick leave,
• aggression, bullying, and intimidation,
• sexual harassment.

Typical adaptation problems of new and marginal workers, shown in:
• sick leave,
• turnover.

Adaptation of the organization to the changing world.

Progress

During this step, it becomes clear to the organization that the idea of 'doing something about stress' is no longer an abstract one. The organization has to invest time and money in it, and those involved have to contemplate a different way of working. Sometimes, this has a shock effect: Isn't the consultant going too far and too fast? Don't we want too much? Isn't it possible to take smaller steps?

When these signals occur, it is important to slow down and not to ignore them. For example, in the beginning people have certain ideas about what a project should be and about who has to do what, and they turn automatically to the consultant. The consultant then has to clarify that they are only in the organization on a temporary basis, and solely to start up the process. A workshop is useful for dealing with ambiguities in the division of roles and possible interventions.

Pitfalls and learning opportunities

The two main pitfalls are the project team becoming too inward looking and the organization losing its motivation.

Insufficient attention to the organization

A stress project can easily become a goal in itself. Both project members and the external consultant tend to isolate themselves and lose sight of what the organization is about. The success of a stress management project is strongly dependent on the way in which consultant and project team are open to the needs and contributions of all parties, in order to realize good communication and relationships. It is crucial to remain connected with the organization, to work together instead of acting alone, to be sufficiently open to the needs, contributions, and resistance of other parties, and not to cling to pre-established approaches.

Loss of interest and motivation

Management or other parties may lose their interest and motivation for the project, for example because of: other problems that demand their attention; problems with communication about the project; underestimating organizational inertia; distrust within the project group or advisory committee.

Point for Reflection
What can you do in order to prevent stepping into these pitfalls? What else might you be able to do in this respect?

Table 4.3: Checklist of outcomes of step 2

Place a cross (X) in the 'Yes' column for each accomplished outcome.

Accomplished outcomes	*Yes*
A further specification of the project	—
Sufficient support for the project in the organization, by incorporating the different parties' interests when goal setting	—
A motivated project team and leader	—
Clear tasks, responsibilities, and powers for team members	—
A clear division of roles between team and consultant	—
Insight into stress among team members	—
Insight into resistance to change and organizational culture among team members	—
A supervisory committee with clear tasks, responsibilities, and powers	—

4.4. STEP 3: DEVELOPING SPECIFIC GOALS

General remarks

Characteristics
If we have successfully dealt with step 2, there should now be sufficient support for the project to set concrete goals. Until now, our efforts have focused on preparing the ground; now we have to decide what we are going to sow and what we will eventually harvest. Step 3 involves setting concrete goals, which offer unambiguous criteria for evaluation, as well as for the choice of the research design and instruments.

An important skill at this stage is the ability to evoke a vision of an attractive organizational future, which can enthuse everybody involved, while at the same time making sure of its feasibility. We also need to be able to co-ordinate the contributions of everybody involved and to avoid, solve, or remove bottlenecks, without losing sight of the final goal. To accomplish this, we have to be able to relate well to diverse people, and unite them in seeking a common goal. This sometimes requires the talents of a stage actor. In step 3, hope is the guiding principle: we focus alternately on an ideal and on the way in which we can maximally achieve this in the organization. The pleasure and motivation here come from being busy together in trying to bring about and design an improvement.

Goal setting
The goal setting specifies the project's intended outcomes and what is necessary for its implementation, as well as the time scale and the budget. The plan contains a global, cohesive, and well-phased review of the project's various activities.

Activities in step 3

In step 3 the following activities occur:

- formulating definitive goals as concisely as possible;
- setting out a phased time path with deadlines for partial activities and budgeting;
- determining an evaluation research design and preparing research;
- composing the measuring instrument for stress risk analysis and letting the supervisory committee test it;
- constructing the other criteria for the project's success;
- making and communicating procedures for dealing with the confidentiality of the research data;
- dividing tasks and responsibilities for the next two phases;
- consulting the supervisory committee;
- feedback of goal setting to the management for authorization;
- making a communication plan (developing newsletters, information packs, etc., all tailored to the organization);
- communicating the definitive goal setting to all parties, preferably with clear support from the management, for instance in workshops;
- educating the project team on all these points (by reading, training, trying things out on each other, and learning by doing).

Goal setting
In step 3, the project team sets shared, unambiguous, and testable goals and develops a vision for the project. These focus on the best possible outcomes for all involved, with sufficient emphasis on feasibility. Subsequently, the team has to communicate these effectively to everybody involved. A popular memory aid here is the acronym

SMART, which reminds us of the criteria 'specific', 'measurable', 'acceptable', 'realistic' and 'specified in time', which we can use to test these goals.

When setting goals, the following areas should be taken into consideration:

- different parties' knowledge level about stress;
- the stress risks;
- effectiveness of work and production;
- pleasure in work and motivation;
- possibilities for development;
- the care system.

Evaluation

Evaluation implies choosing or developing unambiguous criteria, by which we can measure the project's effects. Often, these are scores on questionnaires that measure a certain concept, but it can also involve information about sick leave or productivity. Because of the present scarcity of well-trained personnel, the turnover ratio has also become a very important measure.

Financial criteria. It often makes sense to express evaluation criteria in terms of money. This allows us to estimate in advance the financial consequences to the organization of decreases in stress, in order to set this against the project's budgeted costs. A favourable result can make a strong argument for the project. A less favourable ratio, for example because of high expenses, provides a good reason to have another and closer look at the project.

Different measurements. In evaluation research, there are generally measurements before and after the intervention to be gauged with the help of scores on an agreed questionnaire and other figures. In addition, there will be a prospective measurement (in which people indicate what scores they expect after the intervention), as well as a retrospective measurement (in which people indicate how they would now score the situation existing before the intervention).

It is often instructive for managers and team members to indicate prospectively the expected average scores on the different variables of various groups of employees before and after the interventions. In a workshop before the real measurements are taken, managers and team members write these figures on a big sheet of paper on the wall and then give their reasons. In a subsequent workshop, after the first or second measurements, we can bring out these sheets again to compare these to the actual results and discuss the discrepancies.

Control group. We recommend simultaneously subjecting a comparable group outside the project to all measurements. This group can serve as a control group to enable us to find out to what extent differences between measurements before and after can be attributed to the intervention effects. It makes sense to use a group that will experience the intervention later on.

Measurement instruments
There are a great number of questionnaires available for measuring stress risks. They measure stress sources and reactions, as well as task, organization, and person characteristics. Good evaluation research demands questionnaires that are tailored to what is important in the project. As every country has its own questionnaires, we do not discuss the specific instruments here.

Task characteristics. Task characteristics influence employees' stress and well-being. We can use instruments about task characteristics to indicate and evaluate job redesign interventions. Unlike other instruments, these are usually applied by experts.

Organization characteristics. Instruments that take stock of organization characteristics give a picture of the strong and weak points of departments and whole organizations, as judged by employees. Often, these instruments are concerned with employees' satisfaction, so low scores on certain scales in certain departments can be a reason for doing further research there. This becomes a matter of observation and interviews with key people and those directly involved. Instruments that measure organizational characteristics can be used for 'survey feedback' – feedback of average scores to the organization, for instance by department. The purpose is to evoke a discussion about what can, and has to be, done better on the measured issues and how this can be realized. These instruments can also be used to benchmark the organization against comparable organizations.

Person characteristics. We can use measurements of aspects of the individual related to stress complaints to find out how these are divided over the organization. Subsequently, we can use the results for further research in specific departments.

Mixed characteristics. Some questionnaires investigate the occurrence of sources of stress in personnel, tasks, and organizations, and the resulting stress and health complaints. We can use these instruments to take stock of stress and health risks, which we can then study further with the help of more qualitative methods such as interviews and observation. Chapter 3 provides a number of checklists of stress reactions and sources with mixed characteristics.

Possible solutions. It is very important not only to ask about what goes wrong, but to give respondents sufficient opportunity to indicate options for improvement and problem solving. We can accomplish this by asking open-ended questions about this after every scale.

Sick leave and other personnel data
Sick leave and other personnel data have to be linked to the data provided by the questionnaire. The organization should provide data for each employee, because sick leave data and other relevant personnel data provided by the organization are usually more reliable than questionnaire data regarding these issues. Table 4.4 gives an overview of such data.

Table 4.4: Sick leave and other personnel data

Name and home address of all employees (for sending questionnaires)
Department where the employee works
The total number of sick leave days over the last 12 months
Sick leave frequency over the last 12 months
Age
Sex
Number of years employed
Number of years in the last job
Job
Job level
Education
Salary scale

Confidentiality
When using questionnaires and personnel data, we have to be very careful about confidentiality, because employees' concern about this may lower response rates considerably. We communicate our methods

of dealing with confidentiality during the presentation of the project, but it is worth the effort to repeat this when distributing the questionnaire. However, we are confronted here by a dilemma about the nature of confidentiality. Most of the time it seems to equate with anonymity. Anonymity has advantages, particularly in an organization where employees do not dare to speak freely because they are afraid of the consequences. This is often the case in organizations with a lot of stress (see the warning in the introduction to this chapter), and it makes sense to keep things strictly anonymous in such organizations.

But anonymity has disadvantages too. By not treating employees as individuals, but as representatives of their kind, we deprive them of their responsibility for what they say and perhaps also of their motivation to think seriously about solutions. We also encourage them to exaggerate issues because they see the chance of attaining improper goals (causing problems for their manager, less hard work, etc.). Moreover, it means that we miss out on all kinds of interesting information (further elaboration of solutions, further information from employees who see problems where others do not). Lastly, it becomes impossible to offer focused help to employees who report problems. The most obvious – though still inadequate – solution to this dilemma consists of presenting employees with a brief outline of the advantages and disadvantages of anonymity, then letting them decide for themselves whether they want anonymous treatment or not, and honouring their wishes completely. In table 4.5 we describe a procedure for guaranteeing anonymity.

Point for Reflection
How would you go about tackling confidentiality and anonymity in your organization?

Table 4.5: Procedures for guaranteeing anonymity

We make all research data anonymous.

We do not provide data that can be related to individuals in the organization.

When groups or departments about which we report are so small that individual employees might be identified, we do not report about these groups as such, but add their results to those of other groups.

Only the external adviser or project leader has knowledge about the list of code numbers and names. After having seen the employees with specific stress risks, we destroy the list.

Pitfalls and learning opportunities

Apart from the possibility of leaving out elements described in this section (e.g. because of time or budget constraints), the most important pitfall during this step is failure of communication with one or more of the other parties. This may arise from being insufficiently open to their needs and contributions, or can be a consequence of inadequate communication of our goal setting and its implications. There is also often a question of conflicts of interest between parties that are not thoroughly explored. The effect of failure of communication is often a decline in some parties' motivation. In such a case, the project runs the risk of becoming isolated and degenerating into an exercise in window dressing. A frequently occurring response then is for the project team to become inward looking and to retreat into the research procedures. This can give rise to an atmosphere of reproach and accusation, and the ultimate failure of the project.

Point for Reflection
What are the obvious things you can do in order not to step into these pitfalls? What else might you be able to do in this respect?

Table 4.6: Checklist of outcomes of step 3

Place a cross (X) in the 'Yes' column for each accomplished outcome.

Accomplished outcomes	Yes
A project in progress with concrete goal setting on the following points:	
– a budget	___
– methods to be followed	___
– outcomes to be aimed at	___
– clear evaluation criteria	___
– a research instrument for stress risk analysis	___
– a research design	___
– a time scale and its stages	___
– individual responsibilities	___
– reporting	___
– clear information and communication about these issues to all parties	___
Supplementary actions and interventions based on expected results are discussed	___
All parties show real interest in the project	___
A properly motivated project team	___
A project team with experience of and knowledge about the issues	___

4.5 STEP 4: DESIGNING INTERVENTIONS

General remarks

Step 4 is about finding, inventing, and improving usable interventions. In this step, the consultant, project leader, and other team members have to make use of their creative qualities and intuition. We also have to integrate the issues in a tactically and strategically sound action plan. Besides knowledge and analytic ability, this requires the ability to anchor the results of the intervention in the organization. The pleasure and motivation stem from attempting to make the best possible intervention plan.

The following criteria can be used as guidelines here.

- outcomes for the target group (e.g. well-being, health, effectiveness, possibilities for further development);
- realizing the desired effects as efficiently as possible;
- further training and developing the project group;
- controlling expenses.

Activities in step 4

The consultant is often the most important author of the intervention plan. Because of experience in this area, the consultant will probably supply most interventions. However, it is important to remember that this is a team process that has to result in commitment and further team development, and not a solo performance by the consultant. Besides practical experience, the team supplies knowledge about the organization and the applicability of interventions there, which can often be incorporated into the intervention's design very profitably. The consultant should not take the team members' contributions as criticism, but as an opportunity to specify their own knowledge about applicability of interventions in divergent organizations. This demands a positively critical attitude from the project team towards the consultant's expertise. If these conditions can be met, we can select the best interventions, try to improve them, and determine how we can deal with possible resistance to a particular intervention.

Involving the project team in the design of interventions is primarily an investment in the development of the project team, which has to continue with and supervise the interventions when the consultant has left. The team members should be able to serve as 'stress consultants' within the organization, who can signal stress risks in time, serve as contact people, and conduct work conferences to bring about new solutions. If they can succeed in facilitating employees' creativity to find new solutions, this is of great benefit. We look at this again in the next section.

Point for Reflection
How might stepping into your most basic personal pitfall (see section 4.1) influence your contributions when it comes to being a team member? How might your personal 'allergies' influence your contributions when it comes to being a team member?

Brainstorming
Brainstorming techniques can be very useful when we are designing interventions. The purpose of brainstorming is developing and improving new ideas, and improving team functioning (team building). It is also a very enjoyable activity, which can generate much energy and laughter. Brainstorming usually takes place in two sessions. During the first session, the group supplies answers and solutions to a question or problem, freely and without embarrassment or self-criticism.

During the second session, we can discover answers to the following questions: What is usable and what is not? Which of the elements in the proposed solutions are usable? How can ideas be combined into better solutions?

If necessary, we can repeat the process several times, with the outcomes of the former sessions forming the point of departure for the next one. We can do this, for example, with the help of questions such as: How can this be done in a more pleasant and motivating way? How can this be done more effectively? How can this be done in a more instructive way? Table 4.7 describes a number of additional techniques.

Table 4.7: Techniques for boosting creativity

Identifying 'group think'. This involves looking at ourselves (the team, the organization) from the perspective of someone else who wants either to ridicule or discredit us when it comes to stress. We can actually ask such a person about this, which can be very illuminating.

Breaking rules and suspending promises. This involves approaching a problem as if certain promises, convictions, and rules do not apply for the moment

and finding out what new insights it provides. In this way we can ask our-selves, for example, what would happen or what we would do if we:
- were completely without conscience
- could break all rules
- were very stupid, or very clever
- did not want to succeed
- wanted to bring about a disaster
- wanted to make things less pleasant, motivating, effective and instructive
- had much less – or much more – time or money
- saw money as a much less or much more important outcome than we see it now
- were or wanted to become more or less powerful
- knew that everybody wanted to cooperate or sabotage things
- lived in a perfect or much worse world.

Inventing other functions of interventions and their possible outcomes.

What else can you do with a specific intervention?

What other desirable and undesirable effects does an intervention have?

How could you reinforce or diminish these effects?

Changing perspectives. This involves taking another party's role or a reversed role, and finding out what new insights this provides. You can also do this through role-play. The question is what would you do if you were (or were not):
- a manager, human resources manager, corporate physician, consultant, project leader, etc.?
- a perfectionist,
- sensitive to others' needs,
- socially skilful,
- creative,
- theoretically oriented,
- practical,
- focused on excitement and new experiences,
- power-oriented,
- focused on keeping a nice atmosphere?

Use of metaphors. Here, we explore the similarities and differences between our project and other organisms, processes, or objects. The question may be: which of their characteristics can we use in our project and interventions (think, for example, of a school of fish, an ants' nest, a beach, a motorway, an elephant, an apartment building, a voodoo doll)?

Apart from making up new solutions, we can also use this approach to dis-cover something about the effects of our solutions. For instance, how would our proposed solutions work out in a different institution, such as: a poison factory, a family household, a hotel, an agricultural firm, a brothel, and a jungle?

Use of oracles. This involves using systems that link answers to questions without any theoretical justification. Examples are consulting the 'I Ching' or tarot cards with reference to a definite question. This is not about ultimate answers, but about new and unexpected ideas and elements that might be relevant to the question and might make us think.

Use of prepared pauses. This involves having special thinking pauses to determine whether that provides answers to a specific question, for example by: suggestion techniques ('Next, we will have a thinking pause and you will notice that you will be able to think very clearly and without any prejudice', etc.), 'focusing' (see Gendlin, 1978: formulate the problem as concisely as possible, put it before you, do not 'enter' it, but concentrate on your bodily feelings, and the images, emotions, and meaning that these bodily feelings evoke), Hendricks' (1998) 'ten seconds technique', more or less like the focusing technique, but then more specifically directed on, successively, our neck and shoulders, throat, chest, and stomach. (For a review of these and similar techniques to boost creativity, see von Oech, 1983.)

Possibly, the content of table 4.7 may seem rather 'soft'. However, we must not forget that these techniques only play a role within the first stage of problem solving. In this stage, it is important to take new routes, and to explore new ideas. In the following sessions, however, the approach is completely different. Here we focus on use and practicalities, and importantly on applicability and 'saleability' within the organization as determined by the organizational culture and resistance. Lastly, we try to implement further improvements.

Pitfalls and learning opportunities

Apart from losing sight of the goals and guidelines, communication problems are the most important pitfall here too. First, problems may occur between consultant and project team when the former is not sufficiently open to the team. There is a risk that the consultant can become isolated in an expert role, act alone, and make originality into a value in itself. As a result, team members may feel themselves less creative and may take a more dependent role, starting a vicious cycle. This can end with a very tired, frustrated, and failing consultant and a powerless team that has not learned a great deal and doesn't know how to function in a better way.

Another pitfall is when project team and consultant lose themselves together in their enthusiasm for ever more elaborate intervention plans. The everyday organizational reality may become less attractive than the ideal reality of the plans, and so team members and consultant become less open to other parties' needs and contributions. The increasing distance between the project team and the rest of the organization then leads to disturbed communication and relationships, which can result in frustration on both sides. The risk of defeatism and diminished motivation then looms: 'This doesn't lead anywhere, this is impractical and foolish, takes too long, etc.' versus 'They just don't understand it, pearls before swine, etc.'.

Point for Reflection
What are the obvious things you can do in order to prevent yourself stepping into these pitfalls? What else might you be able to do in this respect?

Table 4.8: Checklist of outcomes of step 4

Place a cross (X) in the 'Yes' column for each accomplished outcome.

Accomplished outcomes	Yes
A set of usable interventions	___
A heightened competence level of the project team	___

4.6 STEP 5: REPORTING

General remarks

Step 5 is about formulating and reporting on the research findings and the resulting advice about interventions to the various organizational parties involved. In step 5, the most important skills are optimally phrasing and communicating results and advice, in a way that is acceptable to the management. This implies insight into technical and content matters, as well as competence in communicating these effectively to the decision makers. The pleasure and motivation comes from attempting to give the best possible advice. Again the guidelines here are the effects on efficiency and effectiveness, job satisfaction and motivation, and possibilities for further individual development.

Activities in step 5

In the former step, the project team acquired sufficient expertise. This leads to the following activities:

- The data of the questionnaire study are entered onto the computer and processed.
- The consultant writes the report, following the guidelines agreed in step 3.
- The consultant reports on the results, first to the project team and, after having incorporated their contributions, to the supervisory committee, which advises about its implications. The project team then jointly analyses the results from the perspective of specifying implications for interventions. It reviews again the interventions from step 4, especially on the following points:
    tracing and filling in gaps (what is still missing?);
  - choices between alternatives;
  - mutual tuning of elements so that they support each other optimally.
- The project team integrates the new information and feedback of the supervisory committee and other stakeholders in a well balanced and suitable action plan for implementing interventions.

Within the project team, the consultant's role can shift to a supervisory one during and after this step. That means that the consultant invites the team to think about its own functioning and its effects, in order to find out what improvements team members can bring about.

The following questions can be of help here:

- What outcomes for the employees (e.g. job satisfaction, well-being and health, options for development) are recognizable in the report?
- How can we realize the desired effects as efficiently as possible with the help of the new information?
- What do the research results mean for the project group's activities?
- Which stakeholders should be contacted first?

- How do the results relate to the interventions we developed in the former step?
- What alternatives are there to the chosen interventions?
- How can we ensure that the different intervention elements support each other optimally?

Furthermore, the project team trains in conducting work conferences by role playing under the direction of the consultant.

Reporting stress risks

Reporting research results

After entering the data onto the computer and performing the statistical analysis, we can start the reporting of stress risks both at the levels of the total organization, and broken down by department, job, age, sex, and so on. The grouping has to be organized in such a way that we can deal with the stress risks found in the groups we distinguish. The most self-evident division is by department, with a further division by job group (e.g. managerial, operational, and supportive). In the reporting, we also indicate what solutions and other options for improvement have been pointed out by the employees. More general analyses, such as comparisons between sexes and age groups on stress risks can also be informative.

Advising

Many complaints about experiences at work indicate stress risks. Complaints might be concerned with the degree of participation, the amount of work, or the relationship with a manager, regardless of stress effects. We interpret a large number of complaints as a signal that something is wrong with the organization, and in such a case our advice is to investigate the way the organization functions and do something about them. This enables us to make the work more effective, pleasant, and motivating, and to improve employees' well-being.

High scores on stress reactions refer explicitly to the presence of stress. When a high level of reported work complaints correlates with high scores on stress reactions, we usually interpret this as an indication of a possible causal relationship (though statistically, correlation does not imply causality). An example is the correlation between many complaints about work or the work environment and high scores on stress effects such as exhaustion. Such a relationship within a particular group of employees, such as a department or employees with similar jobs, enables us to give specific advice for dealing with the factors at their source.

When stress reactions accompanied by complaints about work correlate with sick leave – which does not imply a causal relationship in itself – the project team points out to the organization that dealing with stress risks may be economically profitable. We can then advise integrating stress risk management into sick leave policy. Here too, it is important to pay sufficient attention to the solutions and improvements that the employees themselves have provided. Table 4.9 describes the contents of reporting the stress risks.

Table 4.9: Reporting of stress risks: contents

Introduction

Explanation about the project's design, time scale, and the place of the research results in the organizational policy.

The immediate rationale for the stress management project, the management's vision for it, and its expected added value.

The composition of the project team and supervisory committee.

Theoretical information about work stress.

An overview of definitions and results of conceptual discussions.

Relationship to other projects or developments within the organization.

An 'itinerary' for the remainder of the report.

Preliminary study

A short description and results of previous discussions with the project team, supervisory committee, and stakeholders.

A short description and results of workshops and information sessions.

Responses of employees or the general public (clients, media) to the information supplied.

A short description and results of the preparatory interviews.

Main study

A description of the research design.

An overview of the response rate, including a breakdown of the response percentages of the different groups reported on.

A sick leave analysis.

An analysis of work stress risks in the whole organization.

An analysis of work stress risks related to sick leave.

A description of work stress risks by department and their relation to sick leave. This description has the following structure:

- an overview of experiences of the work and work environment;
- an overview of scores on stress reactions;
- an overview of sick leave;
- a description of relations between work experiences, stress reactions, and sick leave;
- the influence of factors that reduce or increase the influence of stress sources;
- an overview of interventions and concrete possibilities for improvement that the employees provide themselves.

Advising

Advising starts with an overview of stress risks. We make the following distinction:

- general bottlenecks not related to stress risks;
- stress risks that have to be reduced in the whole organization;
- stress risks that have to be dealt with within a certain department and/or group of jobs.

Advising must be concrete and feasible. For each stress risk that we describe, we also give a description of what the various actors (managers, employees, human resources, the project team members and leader) and the supporting parties (consultant, welfare worker, occupational health service, and other care systems) can do. In the Addendum, we give an overview of possible interventions. So this is about: advised measures and intervention; the coherence between results, intended policies, organizational goals, and planned interventions; a time scale for supplementary actions.

Generally, the first activity consists of a workshop at departmental level with a team member and the consultant, or with two team members, as facilitators. In this workshop, feedback of the research results takes place, and we then investigate causal relations, possible interventions by department members themselves, further interventions and so on (for further descriptions see section 4.2 above and the Addendum, section 2).

Partial reports to the supervisory committee and management

In general, it makes sense to present the various parts of the report orally, as soon as they are finished, to the parties involved, and to ask for comments. Most of the time, this is the project leader's task, but the other team members can also do this. The supervisory committee's role is especially important here. It comments on the reports from its own knowledge of the organization, which facilitates a better understanding of the conclusions and what is going on in the organization, as well as creating support for the recommendations.

Though the supervisory committee and management know that many things are wrong – that was the reason for starting the project in the first place – they are still often disappointed by the research results. This is not always the case, but it is important to take this possibility into account. Members of the supervisory committee and stakeholders often cast doubt on the research results, which can result in the actual advice being side-tracked.

Though the research design and measurement instruments have been decided in consultation, it is not unusual for the following comments to be heard: 'The study isn't representative or reliable'. 'Things are completely different in my department.' 'The methods used aren't objective', 'No wonder, when you only ask what's wrong' (or 'This is all much too negative'), 'This is all because of ...' (and then follows a story about somebody with a very bad influence, or a report of an influential event), 'That's only to be expected when everything's anonymous; they feel free to play dirty tricks on you', 'I'm not always happy either, but that's no reason to...', 'Let's get real, these people are not used to.../complain about everything/are much better off here than at ... (another organization)', etc. We encounter again the phenomena of denial and resistance, described in sections 2.1 and 2.2, and here fuelled by feelings of disappointment and hurt among managers and members of the supervisory committee. The poor well-being of the employees exposes the failure of policies, and the old gap between management and workers opens up again. All this makes for a pitfall, especially because the project team has invested much effort and time in the research, and so can often respond in a defensive way when it meets with this kind of criticism. That is why it is important that the project leader or consultant points out this possibility in advance and possibly even lets the team members prepare for it by role playing with each other.

To prevent an impasse, it is important that, in cases of disappointment with the results, members of management and the supervisory committee acknowledge and experience this as such. If the situation allows this, the consultant can act as a kind of group therapist, using approaches such as: 'How do you feel now?'. 'Am I right in thinking that you're feeling something like disappointment/ sorrow/anger?', 'If I'm completely honest, I'd feel rather miserable in your situation too', 'If I believed that I'd done my best and was confronted by something like this, words such as "ingratitude" and maybe even "treason" would come into my mind, even if I knew that it probably didn't make sense. How do you feel about that?'

The danger is that the process can end when we don't acknowledge the disappointment. In that case, consultant and project leader should ask for a new meeting with the same people. Here they can review what has happened and what this means. In addition, we can indicate the importance of good progress, the expectations of the employees, the expenses already incurred, the costs of damage to the project, and so on. Only when the group in question has worked through the disappointment sufficiently, can the project leader or consultant attempt to enthuse them again, and the actual process of advising is resumed. It may help to revert to the expectations they have expressed about the results in the workshop described in step 3.

Pitfalls and learning opportunities

Here again, the main risk consists of communication problems. We have already discussed communication problems with the supervisory committee and management stemming from doubt about the research and its results. Apart from the possibility of impasse, other consequences may be insufficient use of these groups' contributions and poor coordination of the reporting with the organization's goals.

Other problems may occur in the communication between the consultant and the project team, which can lead to loss of energy and enthusiasm in the team. Incomplete communication of results to the work site and delays in reporting can play a role too. Inadequate attention to solutions and improvements proposed by the employees themselves may also be an important pitfall.

Point for Reflection
What are the obvious things you can do in order not to step into these pitfalls? What else might you be able to do in this respect?

Table 4.10: Checklist of outcomes of step 5

Place a cross (X) in the 'Yes' column for each accomplished outcome.

Accomplished outcomes	Yes
A summary of the project's immediate cause, goals, progress, and results	___
Reporting about the results of interviews, questionnaire study, and workshops	___
Insight into the project's progress and outcomes in the supervisory committee and management	___
Understanding about the implementation of follow-up interventions in the supervisory committee and management	___

4.7 STEP 6: IMPLEMENTATION

General remarks

In step 6, we implement the plan based on the research results, which we have decided on together with all the parties involved in step 5. Generally, this is a matter of:

- workshops focused on development of measures, policy, and specific interventions;
- supporting outcomes of workshops (measures and policy);
- implementation, supervision, and further development of possible follow-up interventions;
- feedback of information to management;
- supervision and further development of the project team;
- elaboration of the division of roles in the team, based on clear expectations and responsibilities of team members;
- further anchoring of the project in the organization, preferably explicitly embedded in the organizational vision and mission.

An important skill necessary for success in this step is the ability to translate the rather abstract plan and guidelines into more concrete actions and activities. Another is the ability to 'read' and explore the division of power and the force field. Willingness and ability to ensure the project's place in the organization are also important here. The pleasure and motivation come from actually making it happen, preferably in the best possible way, and also so that the project becomes a permanent part of the organization. The central value for this step is the faith that it is possible to change the present situation in the direction of the vision and goals chosen. An attitude characterized by caution, patience, focus on feasibility, and avoiding pitfalls is important here. We should also be willing to put a lot of attention and effort into an optimal implementation.

Activities in step 6

During step 6, the consultant starts out by supervising workshops, each time with a different team member. One of the purposes is to devise measures and policies, together with the department's employees, to improve the way the organization functions so that it no longer becomes a source of stress. We also take stock of which further interventions are necessary and possible. Another aim is for the consultant to coach and supervise each team member involved in conducting a workshop. Team members will already have been trained in conducting workshops in the earlier step, but now they need to be trained to conduct further workshops in twosomes. During step 6, the consultant's role changes from coach to supervisor. Though the consultant can play a part in implementing some of the follow-up interventions, he or she gradually transfers the implementation to the project team.

The most important task for the consultant now is to ensure that the team actually brings about changes. When this does not happen, or when it happens too slowly, it is of course important to find out why. Often it is because of employees' considerations and feelings comparable to those of the management when it questions the research results. Here too, it often concerns disappointment about the fact that their ways of working and problem solving until now were not effective. This can also play a role among team members themselves, so the consultant first has to discuss this with them. Only when these feelings have been worked through successfully can the team members in turn raise this in the organization.

The consultant's tasks include that of ensuring that team members remain open to the organization and don't primarily focus their attention on each other. Though the latter attitude may feel cosy, it is a sure way to ruin the project. As a supervisor, the consultant enables the team members to perform optimally, without interfering in their performance. The emphasis is increasingly on stimulating autonomy. After all, it is the organization's own responsibility to bring about and anchor the intended changes. If necessary, the consultant should point that out.

In the first instance, the consultant just mirrors the team's questions as much as possible: 'What do you think about it yourselves?' 'If you were very smart, what would you do then?' 'That could work, but how could you do it better/more pleasantly/more instructively?'

In addition, the consultant and team leader occupy themselves with: identification and anticipation of bottlenecks and pitfalls, and ensuring that the team develops procedures for dealing with these; the mutual relationships in the team; allowing the team to adjust to the division of roles; developing a form of time management for the team members, which allows them to give most of their time to the most important issues.

The role of the project team in the implementation

During this step, the project team gradually gains more responsibility. After the workshops, the team ensures that all agreed measures, policy changes, and interventions are actually carried out. Also, they record to what degree this leads to the desired results and whether adjustments are needed. Essentially, this is about safeguarding a high quality project, tailored to the organizational needs, which at least pays for its own costs and strives for added value for the organization. In addition, it is preferable for project team members to play a part in implementing further interventions.

Point for Reflection
When it comes to transferring responsibilities, what would be difficult for you as a consultant?

When it comes to transferring responsibilities, what would be difficult for you as a team member?

The role of other stakeholders

Other employees can also play a part in the interventions. The more an organization can see to its own needs the better. Corporate welfare workers, members of the supervisory committee, line managers, occupational health professionals, human resources officers, and employees at the work site can play an important role in giving information, coaching, or training on the job. The project's outcomes can also be the impetus to take a closer look at the occupational health service or organizational consultancy firms and improve cooperation with them. The human resources department, for example, may develop policies and provisions (for instance in the area of training and job redesign) to solve problems in some groups of employees. Options for interventions are described in the addendum. When the organization's own competence in this respect falls short, of course, external expertise can be called upon.

The relationship between working in projects and organizational policy

As mentioned in section 4.2, a project is a good approach to stress management for several reasons. However, the transition from a content oriented to a more administrative and supervisory role for the project team (see section 4.7) can evoke problems because of the fact that the team acquires a responsibility that in most organizations is a managerial one. This too is mainly a matter of open communication, and workshops about division of tasks, responsibilities, and powers, in which those directly involved reach an agreement, are a good means to this end.

A final issue is that the project team's disbanding may mean that the management of the project dissolves too. That is why it is only logical to incorporate it in another division of management, for instance the organization's overall occupational health policy. It is important to anchor it further by having regular internal audits or stress risk analyses (e.g. within a regular occupational health audit) and specifying goals in this respect (in terms of sick leave, well-being, and employees' experiences of work).

Pitfalls and learning opportunities

There are many kinds of problems at this stage. Problems can occur with the division of tasks, partly because the consultant is now taking another role, which may make the team members feel that the consultant has abandoned them. Moreover, the team members are often too focused on avoiding errors. Sometimes, this acts as a self-fulfilling prophecy, which can create practical problems in workshops and follow-up interventions. When team members do not communicate about this properly among themselves, this can lead to loss of energy and enthusiasm, forgetting the guidelines, and dealing inadequately with mishaps, obstacles, delays, and failures.

In addition, it may be the case that: we have not fully taken into account the solutions and improvements contributed by the employees themselves; those at the top of the organization are not sufficiently involved in implementing further interventions, which may result in too much dependence on line managers; there is inadequate support from the occupational health service; the room for manoeuvre within the organization is too small or the employees concerned show little interest in interventions. All this is usually an effect of poor communication during the previous steps. So improving communication is the main solution.

Point for Reflection
What are the obvious things you can do in order not to step into these pitfalls? What else might you be able to do in this respect?

Table 4.11: Checklist of outcomes of step 6

Place a cross (X) in the 'Yes' column for each accomplished outcome.

Accomplished outcomes	*Yes*
A well coordinated and properly running project	___
Reduction of the consultant's role to supervising from a distance	___
Integration of the project in the organization so that it can function properly	___
Regular contact between the team and the organization's decision makers	___
A team that has undergone a successful transition	___
– and now is properly and autonomously functioning	___
– has clear new ideas about objectives	___
– has divided its tasks sensibly	___
– has a clear focus on the future	___
– has established good internal and external communication	___
– and has a form of intervention running effectively	___
Agreements about the implementation of follow-up interventions	___

4.8 STEP 7: EVALUATION

General remarks

Step 7 is about the project's evaluation. Here, attention is focused on the post-test and the comparison with what has happened with the control group. However, though we treat evaluation here as the final step, it is obviously a process that should take place during the whole project. This step is also concerned with the well-being and health of everybody involved. This means that we must put ourselves imaginatively in the positions of all these other people, from a perspective that focuses on making the changes independent of the individual team members, without losing sight of the goals formulated in step 3.

An important skill here is lateral thinking: being able to see connections between things and processes that others do not see. Another important ability is empathy, looking at the world from the perspective of the other. The motivation stems from the pleasure of improvement and dealing with the results of the project. The guiding principle here is improving effectiveness, in the sense of creating solutions. Ideally, this is done from a position of knowledge and overview of the whole project, knowing what was wrong when the project was at step 1 and what can still go wrong now.

Functions of evaluation

Evaluation focuses on improving the project, but is also strategically important in demonstrating the project's added value. As such, evaluation is a part of knowledge management: by looking closely at the procedures and recording their results, the organization gains a knowledge advantage over the competition. Evaluating is also important when there is a threat that the project will lose its importance, for example, when other issues become more prominent. Evaluation research can then focus attention anew on the necessity for complementary actions to remove bottlenecks. The evaluation must continue to follow the project's progress critically, focusing on permanently improving content quality and adapting to changing circumstances.

Evaluation can focus on the following points:

- the goals of the project;
- the effectiveness of the workshops and follow-up interventions;
- the effectiveness of measures taken by the employees themselves based on the workshops;
- cooperation in the project team;
- the whole process, namely issues such as:
  - the time scale,
  - cooperation and involvement from the management,
  - the involvement and cooperation of the employees;
- the critical incidents and main bottlenecks during the project;
- identifying undesired side-effects;
- useful insights into stress management, from practice as well as theory (more specifically: recording and keeping accessible what the team has learned from literature, symposia, conferences, and talks with professionals and experts from other organizations).

Project evaluation by the consultant

The consultant concludes their contribution to the project by means of a report to the management, written in consultation with the project team. The following points should be reviewed:

- the outcomes and costs of the project, the degree to which the proposed goals have actually been attained;
- the project's place in the HRM policy of the organization;
- action and attention points in the short and medium term;
- the project team members' role within the organization as stress and stress management consultants;
- the role of the consultant and the occupational health service in the short and medium term (e.g. in follow-up studies of stress, meetings with the project team, issues in social-medical meetings, referral in the case of an individual with stress symptoms, etc.).

Again, one of the most important points here is that the consultant emphasizes the comparative advantage that the project has brought about.

Pitfalls and learning opportunities

The following pitfalls and learning opportunities can occur during the evaluation process:

- getting stuck in a 'just good enough' solution;
- negating problems and possibilities for improvement;
- generalizing from incidents;
- project members wanting to implement too many changes in quick succession, having a too theoretical approach that loses sight of practical feasibility, and subsequently retreating into an 'ivory tower' when we don't get what we want;
- diminishing of the project team's activities (becoming mentally lazy, just going through the motions, ignoring the guidelines, sometimes because other matters are more pressing);
- neglecting the project's completion, which results in a damaged relationship between organization and consultant (and their firm) and means that the organization will seek another consultant in case of future problems.

Point for Reflection
What are the obvious things you can do in order not to step into the above-mentioned pitfalls? What else might you be able to do in this respect?

Table 4.12: Checklist of outcomes of step 7

Place a cross (X) in the 'Yes' column for each accomplished outcome.

Accomplished outcomes	*Yes*
Ways of dealing with stress risks, deeply anchored in the organization and specifically tailored to the organization's needs and possibilities	—
Ways of dealing with stress risks which the competition cannot copy easily	—
A specification of outcomes and added value of the whole project	—
Insight into and enthusiasm for the project among all parties	—
Adjustments of the project focused on continuous improvement	—
Project team members who serve as stress consultants	—
A good completion of the project	—
A sound basis for further cooperation between consultant and organization	—

Addendum: Interventions

1 INTRODUCTORY REMARKS

What can we do about stress? In this addendum, we outline some possible interventions. In the following order, we deal with:

- workshops,
- coaching,
- employee assistance programs,
- adjusting the amount of work per employee,
- job redesign,
- career interventions,
- training,
- individual counselling,
- stress consultants.

Most of these are specific applications of HRM interventions that by themselves are not designed especially and uniquely for the management of stress.

Before describing these specific interventions, we want to emphasize the importance of coherence between different interventions at varying organizational levels, not only when alongside each other but in relation to the organization and department's occupational health policy, personnel policies and culture. A well-orchestrated approach in this respect reinforces the impact of any interventions. Though this seems an obvious approach to suggest, coherence in dealing with stress is hard to find in most organizations. Many interventions are chosen and implemented on an *ad hoc* basis. Different parties make up their own solutions, often by hiring different external consultants, resulting in inconsistencies and idiosyncrasies. As a result, the organization itself does not get a grip on its problems. In addition, due to the still existing taboo on stress, open discussions with regard to stress problems and solutions, and hence learning from each other, are unlikely in most departments.

2 WORKSHOPS

2.1 In general

In section 4.2, we described workshops as meetings of existing groups aimed at composing a plan to deal with a certain question. Workshops focus for example on the following issues:

- Clarifying roles and expectations.
- Specifying goals (goal setting) and strategy.
- Improving communication by creating a better structure for deliberation, within and between groups.
- Solving conflicts between individuals and between groups.
- Teambuilding, also in the context of integration of groups with diverging backgrounds, such as in a merger.
- Implementing changes properly, without unnecessary tensions and negative emotions, starting from thoroughly taking stock of (im)possibilities and problems to be expected.

The objective of each workshop is to reach agreements ('So from now on, you will… and I shall…') and to record these. We can then use these as self-evident guidelines in everyday matters, which do not need commenting upon as long as they function properly and do not need adjustment. Possible adjustments can be subjects for a follow-up workshop.

Workshops usually take place somewhere outside the organization. They take a day, a half-day or sometimes two days. Workshops are presided over by one or two facilitators. Facilitators can be project team members or external stress management experts with sufficient organizational knowledge and know-how. Usually, workshops are preceded by interviews with key participants. Apart from the fee for an external consultant, the main costs stem from the fact that the participants are not doing their jobs at that moment. Lastly, there are the costs of the location and catering.

As mentioned in section 4.5, we can also employ brainstorming techniques, as well as other exercises and games. Examples of

exercises and games are simulation and role playing, with or without video-feedback, in which some delegates role-play a difficult situation, while others act as observers. In the subsequent discussion,
the players talk about how they felt, which effects certain actions
evoked and how this could have been done differently or better. The
observers then describe what they have perceived and may give
suggestions for improvement.

Sometimes, it is useful to let role-players exaggerate certain acts
or even complete roles on purpose ('That hand movement there,
how about making it bigger', or: 'Show us what it looks like when
you really overdo it'). Another option is letting players reverse roles
('We are going to do this again, but now you are X and you play Y').
Aside from the fact that this often leads to hilarious results, it also
can lead to all kinds of insight into one's own and others' thoughts
and unwanted effects that we can have on each other. This offers an
entry to adjusting our way of thinking in a way that everybody
involved can subscribe to. In this way, a new reality may come into
being, which all participants experience as something of their own.
This reality enables us to work in a more effective, pleasurable and
instructive way. Essentially, this is about establishing 'dialogue', a
procedure developed by David Bohm, described in Peter Senge *et al.*
(1996).

Successful workshops lead to a concrete division of roles and
tasks. Participants can put themselves forward for the tasks and
roles most appealing to them. In this way, they can use the differences between them productively in order to complement each
other. As a result, synergy may occur. If these tasks and responsibil-
ties, assigned to various individuals, are recorded in writing, they
can serve as points of departure in the future.

Workshops are not limited to a certain organizational level: they
can be conducted at each level. In the remainder of this section, we
give some examples.

2.2 Workshops for the highest level – senior management

In stress management workshops for senior managers and directors,
we can strive for the following objectives.

- Developing a mission ('What is our purpose in the area of
  stress?') and vision ('Where do we want to be, based on our mission, x years from now'), with explicit attention to effectiveness,
  pleasure and development.

- Becoming aware of their own modelling function and its consequences for their own behaviour. After all, all eyes tend to be
focused on the leader and it is impossible not to act or communicate.
- Elaborating how they can propagate their mission and vision
effectively ('Which become our action points in this respect and
which are the consequences of our everyday conduct?'). When
they have become aware of this, they may ask themselves how
they can see to it that they actually will do this.
- Finding and having at their disposal sufficient means and staff
resources to realize a project.

Essentially, this is about strategic thinking: defining a desirable state,
setting concrete goals and determining what has to happen to attain
these goals. Those involved map the options in this direction, as well
as the limitations in the organization and its environment. Next, they
try to get a picture of the causal factors underlying the status quo
and the relations between these. Then, they try to come up with
methods to realize and improve the main options, and to take away,
avoid or neutralize possible hindrances. A simple method to this
end is tracing the worst bottleneck in the work processes at that
moment and then finding out how one might deal with it. The next
step is determining the possible undesirable effects that such an
intervention may cause. This allows them to adjust the interventions
to prevent or neutralize possible undesired effects, or to go in a completely different direction.

   This can lead to a well-orchestrated and well-instrumented
master plan, which specifies the people needed, financial means and
methods. Such an approach also enables one to go on distinguishing
between main and side issues and to act accordingly. This boils
down to delegating properly, creating proper conditions and not
losing oneself in operational and unnecessary work, both before and
after the execution of interventions. To illustrate the course of affairs
further and offer exercise material, one can make use of case studies.

2.3 Workshops to create appropriate conditions for stress management

Policies to create appropriate conditions in the area of preventing
and taking away stress are a personnel, occupational health and line
management responsibility. In order to result in effective changes,
such policies must come about in close consultation between these

two parties. This implies that in workshops on this subject both the personnel and occupational health officers and relevant line managers have to be present. Such workshops can for example focus on the following subjects.

- Jointly optimizing on the one hand effectiveness and quality of production (for example by optimizing workflow) and on the other hand the well-being and health of everybody involved.
- Optimizing organizational transparency so that all employees know which options the organization is offering and which consequences different lines of conduct imply.
- Optimizing internal communication, between management and work-site, as well as between and within departments. In this way, the organization can diminish, for instance, insecurity about the future by giving proper information. Issues may be related to expected developments, as well as intended changes and reorganizations, and their consequences. This can be done in discussions of progress or special plenary meetings, or by a corporate video – journal, circulars and e-mail.
- Further developing the organization's own human resource management strategy. This can be for example a matter of policy-making for:
  – selection,
  – training and education,
  – coaching,
  – career guidance.
- Optimizing leadership at the different levels.
- Further developing the occupational health policy, for example by conducting periodic occupational health studies and risk analysis, and providing fitness facilities.
- Introducing or extending day-care facilities for small children.

2.4 Workshops on implementing change

Implementing change usually evokes resistance, even when there is a thorough plan that stems logically from the organizational mission and vision. This applies also to changes that, in theory, provide only positive outcomes for all parties, such as interventions to prevent stress. In order to implement a well-supported change project, an implementation workshop should consist of the next steps.

- Identifying all parties.
- Discussing the 'unspeakables' in this area.
- Learning about the interests of all parties involved in the changes, as well as of hindrances and options that each party sees.
- Bringing to the surface the opinions and thoughts underlying each of these scenarios.
- Trying to adjust and integrate the opinions of the different parties, in order to bring about 'and–and' solutions by creating a commonly shared and sufficiently supported picture of solutions and causes of the existing problems.
- Coming to concrete agreements and recording these.
- Follow-up.

2.5 Workshops on communication between departments

Poor communication between departments can lead to disturbance of the smooth progress of tasks, characterized by alternating periods of work overload and forced inactivity. Such problems can become more intense in the case of conflict between department managers and mutual rivalry of departments. In these cases, communication can be improved by holding a work conference with representatives from both departments. The following issues then can pass in revue.

- Improving communication for example by:
  - discussing and recording mutual expectations,
  - tracing and discussing 'unspeakables',
  - keeping communication open (for example: not 'throwing things over the fence', warning in time for delays and big amounts of work that can be expected).
- Solving problems between group and departments or making them less vicious, by dealing with distorted perception, prejudice and stereotyping.

2.6 Workshops for problems within departments or teams in general

There are all kinds of problems within groups that can give rise to disturbances of work processes. We can solve some of these by workshops that bring about a culture change. Successively, we pay attention to the following processes.

- Mergers and reorganizations.
- Changes focusing on better attuning to the environment.
- Joint optimizing of production and well-being.
- Cleaning up an unpleasant past.
- Calming down a 'stress culture'.
- Solving conflicts and poor communication and improving social support.

2.7 Mergers and reorganizations

To introduce, structure and implement mergers or reorganizations, we can think of workshops to consolidate a new mission and vision at the level of the department or team. The purpose can also consist of getting a better look at the greater picture, namely the department's role in the organization and the organization's place in its environment, to clarify the meaning of their own contribution. Realizing the mission and vision at the level of the department and the individual can then result in guidelines for independent, strategic and tactical thinking and acting. These guidelines enable those involved to determine for themselves which tasks have priority and which have not. In addition to giving employees more insight, it also ensures that they need less managing.

When there is no well-defined mission, it is also crucial to organize workshops at a department level in the case of radical reorganizations and mergers. This makes it possible to create more quickly a new and functional reality, shared and subscribed to by everybody involved (more or less as described in section 2.4). A useful entry here is to let everybody outline the strong and weak points of each of the department's 'constituent parts'. Along these lines, it is then possible to create an 'improved' reality by further strengthening strong points and counteracting and compensating for the effects of the weaker points. This leads then to explicitly recorded expectations and obligations of all employees involved. Especially in the case of mergers in which departments are actually integrated, this should be an obligatory part of procedures. Only then, one has a chance to prevent mutual stereotyping, prejudice and mistrust that may determine, if not poison, the working climate for as long as the present employees are around.

2.8 Changes focused on better attuning to the environment

The organization's attuning to its environment can show flaws in the absence of any merger or reorganization also. This is related to the rapid succession of changes in our world, mentioned in the introduction. Workshops can contribute to cultural changes leading to better attuning. Organizational culture refers here to the fixed ways in which the organization's employees solve their ever-recurring problems, what they say about it and what they think and feel in the process.

Changes in this respect tend to be hard to implement as long as the culture is good enough to keep things operational. In a quickly changing environment however, a culture can become too limiting and give rise to all kinds of bottlenecks. Adjustment then is necessary if the organization wants to survive. Here too, an important aid can consist of making the organizational mission and vision concrete at the level of the department: what do mission and vision imply to this department?

2.9 Joint optimizing of production and well-being

In workshops at the departmental level, we can also focus more specifically on designing and implementing changes to jointly optimize production and well-being. Workshops are a very important instrument in this respect (see chapter 4). People can for example decide to deal with the major constraints by technological interventions and employing more people. Also we can pay attention periodically to looking for improvements, for example in brainstorming sessions about certain sides of the department's work. Moreover, we can devise standard procedures to handle unexpected emergencies. Lastly, we can use workshops to come to agreements on specific interventions such as job redesign, training – on the job or not – and coaching.

2.10 Cleaning up an unpleasant past

When an organization in its past has evoked much resentment, dissatisfaction and frustration in many employees, this often leads to a collective attitude of indifference, mistrust and cynicism. In such a case, it is often useful to find out in workshops what has happened. This boils down to discussing 'unspeakables', raking up old conflicts, bringing up what is swept under the carpet and opening closets within which everybody involved knows, or suspects, are housed 'old skeletons'.

In addition to all parties involved having to muster considerable courage to this end, there has to be sufficient trust that the organization is willing to actually do something about the points that show up. To achieve this, we must allow the nasty events from the past to 'get' to us sufficiently. This enables us to give these events their deserved place in the common organizational history and to free ourselves from their influence. Only then are we able to occupy ourselves with some faith in a better future. In mutual discussion, we can determine then how we shall continue, without passing over what has happened. An excellent manual in this respect is *Driving Fear out of the Workplace* by Kathleen Ryan and Daniel Oestreich (1991).

2.11 Calming down a 'stress culture'

A 'stress culture', that is an organizational culture in which the members 'infect' each other by their haste, tension and other stress phenomena, provides another reason for conducting a workshop. People do not differ in this respect from other mammals that live in groups (see section 3.1). It often occurs in organizations where deadlines play an important part and those involved have to respond quickly to changing circumstances (editorial offices of journals, advertising firms, TV studios, see the examples of too little orderliness in section 3.2). In such a case, we first must make things perceivable and discussible. This then becomes the point of departure from which participants have to devise and safeguard new ways of working.

2.12 Solving conflicts and improving poor communication and social support

Other forms of culture change by means of workshops take place in the case of problems with stress stemming from conflicts and poor communication and social support. Depending on the specific problems, we can use workshops to try to achieve the following goals.

* Keeping open communication channels. The purpose here is that those involved do not withhold data and opinions any longer: they must identify the 'unspeakables', in order to discuss those after all (see section 2.2).

- Role clarification, for example in the case of changes accompanied by shifts in responsibility, other forms of role ambiguity and avoiding responsibilities.
- Developing standard procedures for turning over work, for example in the case of individual task overload, holidays, sick leave, part-time employees and sudden emergencies that demand full attention of one or more employees and interfere with the normal course of affairs.
- Developing standard procedures to break in temporary employees and to try to make them into 'regular' temporary employees or 'stand-by employees'.
- Implementing and structuring work progress meetings.
- Solving conflicts, for example by 'making the pie bigger' and creating 'win–win' solutions.
- Preventing and dealing with bullying at work, as well as stereotyping of certain groups, based on sex, age, social class, ethnic or regional background, or religion.
- Teambuilding, focused on mapping and using differences in skill and personality to attain more synergy (for a further elaboration, we refer to Stephen Covey's book, 1989).
- Implementing one or more of the following interventions, such as job redesign, training – 'on the job' or not – and coaching.

In all cases, we can find out in workshops what is going on, on which suppositions everything is based and how we can change things. Once again, the guidelines are making work more effective, pleasurable and instructive. Once we get to agreements, we record and implement these. After some time, we evaluate these and make adjustments.

3 COACHING

'Coaching' here means that a manager, who is confronted by stress problems in her or his organization or department, calls upon an external expert. At the same time, the manager remains completely responsible for his or her own decisions and interventions. The coach is just an independent discussion partner from outside the organization. Of course, the costs of this approach are relatively low.

The coach's attitude and role may vary. So he or she can alternately serve as:

- listening ear,
- sparring partner,
- 'motivator',
- devil's advocate,
- individual trainer,
- psychotherapist,
- stress expert,
- organizational consultant,
- actor who plays the role of someone from the organization in role playing,
- strategist and tactician,
- court jester,
- table companion, etc..

On the one hand, the coach brings sufficient expertise, as well as tactical and strategic skills in the area of stress in organizations, and can contribute to the design and implementation of interventions. In addition, such a person has insight in intrapersonal processes, and he or she even serves, to a certain degree, as a kind of psychotherapist to mentally healthy persons who are relatively free of psychological complaints. Seeking a coach is not a sign of weakness, but a matter of wanting to perform optimally and develop oneself. In coaching, the following elements play an important role.

- Asking questions, focused on clarifying problems, goals, strategy, tactics and pitfalls, both of a technical and a personal nature.
- Other counselling techniques, such as mirroring, summarizing, consolidating, meta-communicating, confronting, etc.
- Brainstorming techniques (see 4.6).
- Tips and advice ('From my own experience, I know that in such a case it is often useful to...')
- Bringing up theoretical knowledge ('According to Mintzberg/ Freud / Marx...' etc.).

Coaching can focus on:

- exploring limitations and possibilities,
- determining a vision and goal setting,
- making, improving and implementing plans,
- avoiding pitfalls, and
- motivating employees.

Though the coach focuses on organizational processes, the coach can also attend to blind spots, blockades, avoidance and forms of undesired automatism of the person to be coached. These blind spots can often be a good reflection of the rules and regulations of the organizational culture.

4 EMPLOYEE ASSISTANCE PROGRAMMES (EAPS)

EAPs originate from America. The programmes are meant to improve the well-being and health of all the organization's employees. As such, EAPs can diminish stress. Though such a programme can be useful, it usually does not deal with the causes of stress, sick leave or psychological complaints as far as these lie within the organization. This makes the rationale somewhat unclear. Generally speaking, however, evaluation studies indicate that EAP outcomes are positive and are more than cost-effective. Examples are programmes and facilities focused on:

- fitness and sports;
- healthier food (also in the works canteen);
- stopping smoking;
- drinking less alcohol;
- using less medicine;
- improving safety at the work-site;
- stress management courses;
- time management courses;
- personal effectiveness courses;
- possibilities for psychosocial counselling and psychotherapy (sometimes by a telephonic emergency service);
- crisis intervention after traumatic incidents;
- corporate welfare work (for example, to take care of ill and disabled family members);
- juridical assistance;
- referring to other specialists, such as physiotherapists and orthopaedists (often within so-called 'back schools');
- corporate crèches.

5 ADJUSTING THE AMOUNT OF WORK PER EMPLOYEE

Though high work pressure is not only a matter of too much work *per se*, it still may occur that employees simply have too much work. Though a different organization of work and other interventions mentioned in this addendum generally can lead to a considerable relief in this respect – and we should look into that first – sometimes this is not sufficient. To meet such problems, the following issues are relevant.

• Sufficient emancipation of department employees: employees should dare to communicate about their problems in this respect and not be driven by fear or inappropriate pride.
• Managers who are open to signs of these problems.
• Sufficient expertise, courage and feeling of responsibility in management to do something about it.
• Good communication with top management.
• Good faith in management.
• Availability of sufficient means.

Dependent on the expected duration of the problem, we then can search for solutions in the following approaches.

• Hiring extra regular and/or temporary personnel (if available), and installing proper procedures to break in new people, without overloading regular personnel in the process.
• Retraining personnel, so that they can step in where and when needed (broadening and enriching tasks).
• Deploying extra equipment and machinery.
• Automating certain parts of the work (while seeing to it that the remaining tasks do not result in impoverished jobs).
• Working overtime, at least when this is a temporary phenomenon.
• Contracting out that part of the work for which the organization itself has insufficient capacity.
• Contracting for fewer orders.

6 JOB REDESIGN

6.1 In general

Job redesign is indicated when the present jobs in themselves are a very important source of stress. Indications may stem from complaints from employees (step 2) and measurement of job characteristics (step 4).

Job redesign starts out by analysing jobs to find out which job parts and characteristics evoke stress. This should be done in a few days. The input of an ergonomist or an expert in the area of work hygiene may be important here. When we have established the bottlenecks, we can look for solutions and start redesigning the job. This, again, is about striving for joint optimizing of employees' effectiveness, pleasure, development and health.

Protagonists of the sociotechnical approach foster the idea that work stress can be attributed primarily to faulty job design. Measures starting from this approach depart from a form of quantifying stress risks in a particular job. This can be, for example, a matter of the work's pace or quantity, or of its difficulty, monotony or meaninglessness. Stress risks can also stem from employees' inability to influence the work environment or task content and insufficient options for interpersonal interaction (see section 3.2).

When we have determined the intrinsic stress risks of jobs, we often can redesign these jobs in a way that leads to better products and contributes to higher quality work processes (in terms of pleasure, effectiveness and options for individual development). Also, it is sometimes possible to attune jobs in such a way that extra manpower is set free to help execute unavoidable heavy tasks. All in all, we can do in this way something about qualitative underoad stemming from meaninglessness, monotony and lack of autonomy, as well as several forms of overload inherent in a job (see section 3.2).

We will describe here a number of options, namely:

- broadening jobs;
- enriching jobs;
- more autonomy;
- more opportunities for social contact;
- autonomous task groups or self-directing teams;
- other interventions in the context of job redesign;
- individualized job redesign.

Though all forms demand some change in the organization at large, different forms of job redesign vary in the amount of change they imply. Some forms only affect one work unit (for instance enriching jobs, more autonomy and more opportunities for social contact) while others demand changes in several departments (broadening jobs) or even the complete organization (in the case of autonomous task groups). Of course, the time path, the resistance to be expected and the implementation costs inherent in the different forms of redesign will vary with the extensiveness of the change. Some individualized interventions can be carried out almost immediately (especially when these are devised by the employees themselves), while the complete implementation of autonomous task groups (from the first proposal to well-balanced, smoothly functioning teams) may take years. In our opinion, job redesign should be introduced always in the context of a workshop, which allows for ventilating objections as well as proposing adjustments and improvements. Moreover, employees should be encouraged to keep account of everything that goes wrong and to think about improvements for later discussion. The main expenses stem from a possible initial decrease of production due to the necessary workshops and extra meetings and discussions, as well as from getting used to the new ways of working. Of course, this is only a temporary phenomenon, which may be more than compensated later on.

6.2 Broadening jobs

Broadening jobs, often linked to some further instruction or training, can sometimes prevent and counteract stress. Broadening jobs implies that an employee performs different tasks. This makes it possible to alternate one-sidedly taxing or very boring tasks with different tasks within one job. This results in more possibilities for recovery and less fatigue. Also, we can prevent rut and monotony in this way. An additional advantage is that, in the case of capacity problems, more people can step in, because more people are able to perform the specific task. It is important, however, that the different tasks are sufficiently related to each other. Examples are:

- alternating visual display unit tasks with different tasks to prevent repetitive strain injury (RSI);
- alternating call centre tasks with different tasks in a banking and assurance firm to deal with the high sick leave among the call centre personnel;

- alternating tasks of drivers, counter clerks and security personnel in a public transport company, to counteract several forms of under- and overload;
- alternating road mender's and gardener's tasks within a municipality to prevent knee trouble for road menders.

6.3 Enriching jobs

Enriching jobs is a specific form of broadening jobs. It is about allowing employees to deliver a more complete product and so to give the work more meaning, which would provide more satisfaction. This implies that employees don't perform exclusively a very narrow partial task anymore, but are engaged also in other partial tasks, such as planning, work preparation, quality inspection, machinery maintenance, troubleshooting, breaking in new employees, etc.

6.4 More autonomy

Job redesign can consist of offering more autonomy, a greater freedom to design and structure our own work, for example in the area of the execution and sequence of different task elements and the timing of pauses. A greater level of participation in decision-making processes is also important in this respect. Having more autonomy can contribute to more independence being experienced and enhanced commitment to the work. Providing sufficient information about the organization and work itself also reinforces the feeling of being able to influence things. The employee has a better grip of the situation and can make better choices. All this can be very important to lighten the experienced task load.

6.5 More opportunities for social contact

Through job redesign, we can also create more opportunities for social contact, social support and sufficient mutual feedback (in some cases by intercom, e-mail or other means). Better communication can be important to task performance, and can also contribute to recovery from fatigue and stress, and increase in work motivation and pleasure. As such, we can consider opportunities to engage in social contact as a form of autonomy. Research shows that social support can play an important role in preventing and counteracting stress. In many simple kinds of work, pleasurable contacts with colleagues also turn out to be the most important positive outcome for the employees involved (see section 3.2).

6.6 Autonomous task groups or self-directing teams

We can achieve many of the above-mentioned interventions by installing autonomous task groups or self-directing teams. In this approach, a team of employees decides itself how it can realize specific targets. As such, it shows some similarities to the concept of a learning organization, while in our own project team approach these principles play a role also. In autonomous task groups, the employees design for themselves ways of working and co-operating without unnecessary task fragmentation. Nowadays, this approach is very popular, in industrial as well as administrative organizations. However, this popularity stems foremost from the favourable effects on production quality and costs, and to a lesser degree from concerns about stress and well-being. For a good manual on how to install and maintain autonomous task teams, we refer to *Why Teams Can Fail and What to do About it* by Darcy Hitchcock and Marsha Willard (1995).

6.7 Other interventions in the context of job redesign

When a job gives rise to role ambiguity, role conflicts or other conflicts – all well-known stress sources – formulating a sound job description can instantly be of help. Also, we can design jobs in such a way that they are characterized by less task disturbance. So we can install fixed times at which we can be called or hire somebody who makes a first selection of our mail and telephone calls. Essentially, these are time-management techniques applied to jobs. Finally, there are, in the context of job redesign, the following other interventions.

- Ergonomic adjustments (an ergonomically sound chair, desk or visual display unit).
- More user-friendly software.
- Automating too simple work.
- Taking out the most demanding task elements or making these less demanding, for instance by ergonomic or technological adjustments. Especially in the case of handicapped employees, such adjustments can help to make work do-able (a better mouse

and/or extra support for the underarm in the case of operating a visual display unit; equipment to lift weights, etc.).
- In the case of monotonous work, if possible, offering opportunities to do something else at the same time (for example, listening to music or training tapes by headphones).
- Introducing game elements in monotonous work.
- Interventions in working times (better dosage of and timetables for irregular shifts; the option of partial jobs; a fixed or a variable amount of working hours; more pauses; flexible working times; study or sabbatical leaves).
- Appropriate safety measures that minimize traumatic events.

6.8 Individualized job redesign

Generally, the above-mentioned interventions work best when we custom-tailor these to employees' individual desires and needs. The following options exist:

- Individualized performance norms, which take into account the individual possibilities and limitations.
- Individualized jobs and working conditions.
- Individualized pay (cafeteria system) and pension plans (earlier or later, complete or partial).
- Individualized work-sites (flexible offices, neighbourhood offices, working at home).
- Individualized working times, allowing us to better integrate work and home front demands.
- Individualized and adjustable furniture and equipment.

7 INTERVENTIONS IN CAREERS

7.1 In general

In the case of preventing and counteracting stress, we can think also of changing careers to attain a better person-job fit and to realize further personal and professional development. As such, this is a normal part of HRM, which makes it difficult to estimate the costs attached to it. Generally speaking, we can say that the gains usually outweigh the costs. Neither can much be said about the rationale for practising such an approach: at the moment, this is simply the most rational approach when the organization perceives its personnel as an important factor in its own survival.

Here too, these interventions work best when we apply these in an individualized way, in order to make the best of somebody's individual talents, motives and career stage. We will outline the following interventions in more detail:

- selection policy;
- career policy;
- interviews about employees' functioning and career;
- replacement;
- job rotation;
- secondment;
- outplacement;
- projects.

7.2 Selection policy

To prevent stress and an inappropriate task load, selection has to focus on a good fit between the persons on the one hand and work and organization on the other. This is, among other things, a matter of talents, abilities and skills of the future employee. Being able to deal with stress can be part of this, at least when this is important for the job in question. Furthermore, proper selection is also a matter of the compatibility of values and norms of the person and organization. The selection procedure is also an excellent opportunity to map somebody's training needs, also when it comes to dealing with stress. For the latter option, we can use a special kind of assessment centre, in which the candidate participates in simulations and role playing meant to find out how that person deals with stress-evoking situations.

Another important issue in selection procedures is a proper scanning of 'organizational psychopaths'. Psychopaths are here referred to as people who, despite which organization they work for, seek only to realize personal goals, at the expense of other people. To spot these individuals, we can look into the history of former jobs, conflicts, people around them who suddenly have disappeared from view, misused subordinates, gaps in their CV, all kinds of sexual affairs etc. The easiest way is to check thoroughly the references they give and contact their former employers.

7.3 Career policy

From a HRM perspective, employees make up the main organizational capital. So it is foolish to expose them to unnecessary stress. For this reason, it is also important to allow them to develop in a way that is optimally attuned to both their own needs, talents and values, as well as the organizational needs and values. To this end, the organization tries hard to meet individual training needs and develop useful individual talents. This approach implies also that the organization enables its members to prepare and make subsequent career steps in time. Coaching and mentoring can be very useful here. It means also that, from time to time, the parties involved have a closer look at the employee's present options, skills and further training needs. This can imply the use of psychometric tests and forms of self-assessment, such as writing an autobiography, for instance in the context of a self-management training programme (see 8.9). A proper insight into the role of the employee in the organizational mission and vision and the policies stemming from these are very important as well. Only then, is it possible to really shape one's own career in a proactive way. In other words, the organization has to be sufficiently transparent.

7.4 Interviews about employees' functioning and career

An important element of career guidance is regularly interviewing employees about their functioning, in which further career development is one of the topics. As well as employee and manager delving explicitly into matters such as stress, they can talk about all kinds of interventions. The following career interventions can be part of this.

7.5 Replacement

One of the options is replacement to a job with different work pace and job demands. Replacement comes up when we want to attain a better person–job fit, while job redesign is impossible and changes from the employee's side are unlikely. This can happen when a job has become too heavy, but also when a job does not offer sufficient challenges anymore. Another reason can be that somebody is not so popular in a certain department and wants to start all over with a clean slate elsewhere. In large organizations, replacement can offer good solutions.

7.6 Job rotation

Job rotation, changing jobs from time to time, an intervention related to broadening jobs, can help to prevent the fatigue, wear and tear, and stress, stemming from continuously doing the same job. An additional advantage as with previously mentioned interventions, is that, if needed, more people can step in, because more people are competent at that task. In general, the outcomes to all parties involved are the highest when the different jobs somehow fit in with each other. Changing merely for the sake of change often makes no sense and usually is not motivating.

7.7 Secondment

Sometimes, it is possible to place employees in other organizations on a temporary basis (secondment). These organizations can be clients or suppliers, but research institutes or universities can be likely candidates also. In addition to being developmental for the employees involved, they can also, as a kind of consultant or 'liaison officer' pass information and wishes to and from both sides, from which all can profit greatly. In the profit sector, we can think, for example, of somebody from a supply firm who helps a client organization to think about the development of new products. He or she can focus there on specification of possible new contributions by the supplier, as well as on new applications of existing products of their own company within the products of the client firm. In the non-profit realm, there are exchange programmes between related organizations to learn from each other, for example between ministries and municipalities.

7.8 Outplacement and lay-off

Sometimes, it is wise to invest in employees' employability by offering specific training programmes to enable them to find a good job elsewhere. This may spare them unnecessary problems and misery, and prevent the expenses of lengthy sick leave or work disability. When lay-off is inevitable, the organization should act so that those directly involved experience the least possible pain and disadvantage. As well as being a matter of simple decency to these employees, it also implies a positive signal to the personnel that remain employed. A considerate approach can prevent the latter group from experiencing feelings of guilt, loss of faith in the organization and de-motivation (the so-called survivors' syndrome).

7.9 Projects

Other options to prevent getting stuck are special temporary projects to attain a certain goal that is important to the organization. Within such a project, the participating employees can contribute their specific skills and knowledge, while they can also develop and broaden themselves further by learning from each other and the process. Also, they can extend their social network. In fact some companies are almost entirely organized around working in projects (which, for that matter, is not the best way to prevent stress). The project teams that have a central place in our own approach can serve this purpose also.

8 EDUCATION AND TRAINING

In this section, we distinguish between education and training programmes for managers and those for other employees. Though education and training can – and should! – also take place at the work-site ('on the job training'), we discuss mainly education and training that takes place elsewhere.

The need for training is indicated in the case of an attitude problem or a lack of skills and knowledge, which hampers the organization in its functioning and/or development. The time and financial means needed for training vary per programme. The costs of training consist mainly of the employees' absence from the work site. In addition, there are the costs of the development of the training (only if it is a custom-tailored programme), its preparation, the actual training hours, (sometimes) the evaluation, location and catering. Most training programmes take from one to five days.

8.1 Training programmes for managers – general remarks

The experienced workload of employees depends to an important degree on the way managers behave. Training or coaching managers in leadership can contribute significantly to employees' stress prevention and reduction. Essentially, guarding the emotional climate is one of the most important managerial tasks. A manager can engage for example in the following activities, which can each be crucially important when it comes to preventing or counteracting unnecessary stress – and can all be taught in a leadership programme.

- Paying sufficient attention to the department and being actively involved with the interpersonal sides of it (this implies also that the manager should not treat the department exclusively as a useful leg up to a next job). Sometimes, however, it may be better to specifically appoint somebody extra to this task. Such a person should then get a sufficient mandate, a form of leadership that we call co-management.
- Trying to act fairly and making that clear, that is, not acting out of self-interest or favouritism.
- Gathering enough knowledge about the department's or team's past (from different sources!) and the problems that occurred in it.
- Really putting problems on the agenda and discussing these in a constructive, problem-solving way in works progress meetings and in individual talks with the people with whom one has difficulties.
- Informing employees as early as possible in face-to face interactions about approaching radical changes (changes in their jobs, replacement, lay-off).
- Discussing things periodically during works progress meetings in times of reorganization and merger. To prevent needless worrying and rumours, it is useful to explicitly ask about rumours during meetings and to comment on these as openly as possible.
- Assisting and protecting one's employees, if needed.
- Offering emotional support, if needed.
- Serving as a coach, who gives his or her employees the neecessary room to function properly, listens to their contributions (also when these imply critique on his or her person) and actually uses these. Apart from creating the proper conditions, this implies stimulation of self-steering and giving advice if necessary.
- Regularly interviewing employees about their individual functioning and career, and, if needed, offering training, coaching or mentoring.
- Showing approval for good performances.
- Being reserved about implementing changes (no changes for the sheer purpose of changing in itself).
- Implementing changes in such a way that it evokes the least negative emotions.
- Giving bad news in such a way that it evokes the least negative emotions.

- Being focused on recognizing task-overload and stress reactions.
- Being focused on recognizing bullying, scapegoating and stereo-typing.
- Keeping in touch with ill employees, preparing their return to the department or team and investing extra time and attention in them after their return.
- Giving extra time and attention to employees who have experienced a traumatic event. Here, it is especially important to let them talk about what they have gone through and to find out whether referral to a specialist is necessary.

Though all above-mentioned points matter in creating appropriate working conditions without unnecessary stress risks, it is especially important for managers to get some extra training in social skills and stress prevention.

8.2 Training in social skills

Training programmes in social skills for managers focus on increasing their sensitivity and authenticity. Keywords are leadership and teambuilding. To create the proper conditions for optimal performance, motivation and learning possibilities, as well as to bring about an atmosphere of good social support, managers need to master the following interpersonal skills.

- Listening skills:
  - empathizing,
  - 'reading' non-verbal behaviour,
  - interviewing skills,
  - delaying responses,
  - responding appropriately to violent emotions,
  - recognizing and acknowledging individual differences,
  - moral sensitivity.
- Other coaching skills:
  - internal congruence (being undivided) and integrity,
  - meta-communicating,
  - showing approval and disapproval,
  - positive re-labelling,
  - helping people to make choices,
  - goal-setting techniques,
  - generating 'win–win' solutions,
  - delegating,

- Other social skills to lead groups:
  - making use of individual differences (synergy),
  - negotiating and conflict management,
  - leading workshops and other meetings (steering on outcomes, list of decisions, etc.).

All this is a matter of instruction, discussion and role-playing, with each other or with actors, where the trainees serve also as observers each time.

8.3 Stress prevention

Training in stress prevention has the following important outcomes.

- Being able to notice stress risks and reactions earlier and better.
- Acquiring a conceptual framework to talk about all this.
- Breaking the taboo on talking about stress at work and talking more easily about it with one's employees.
- Knowing about stress effects and their costs.
- Having some knowledge about interventions.
- Implementing interventions in one's own unit.
- Dealing with crises and traumatic events (hold-ups, accidents, lay-offs, etc.).
- Knowledge about options of referral.
- Mapping one's own stress sources and reactions, and their underlying causal patterns.
- Dealing better with one's own stress and be a role model in this respect.

The scores on a questionnaire about stress sources and reactions in one's own organization or department makes a good entry point for such a training programme. Here, too, it is important to get a lot of actual practice, in terms of role-playing and in real life, and to give and receive a great deal of feedback.

8.4 Training programmes for individual employees – in general

To prevent and deal with stress, different kinds of training programmes for individual employees can contribute positively. Here too, the contribution is greater relative to the degree that the training fits in with the employees' own wishes and needs. So participation always has to be based on an agreement with or a request from the individual employee. We outline the following forms of training.

- General education.
- Technical and professional training – also for employees over forty.
- Training in personal effectiveness or assertiveness.
- Training in counteracting stereotyping and bullying.
- Training in time management.
- Training in self-management and employability.
- Training in stress management
- Ergonomic training.

8.5 General education

Sometimes, someone has sufficient potential to work at a much higher level, but at the same time, for all kinds of reasons, his or her education is insufficient. In such a case, it makes sense to enable such an employee to follow a tertiary education. In this way, we may accomplish a better person–environment fit, prevent de-motivation and loss of interest, and make better use of someone's talents.

8.6 Technical and professional training

Supplementary technical and professional training can help employees to perform their tasks in such a way that these no longer evoke stress. In addition, such training can help employees to qualify for jobs that are more appropriate to them. Furthermore, additional training may be called for when tasks and jobs are changed, for example in the context of a reorganization. In principle, all kinds of professional training can play a role here. This applies also to on-the-job training, within or without the context of a learning organization.

A special case consists of short programmes to get acquainted with a new computer system or programme. These are often omitted, based on the mistaken supposition that these are superfluous, because people will learn this in everyday practice anyhow. However, some good instructions, that specifically go into the differences with the former system and the new options that the new system offers can make a serious difference.

Though technical and professional training can be very important to prevent and solve problems of employees over forty, these employees also often get insufficient complementary training. To improve this, an organization may offer them a varied menu of relevant and accessible programs and courses, from which these employees too may choose. To these older employees, good discussions in this respect with managers and personnel and occupational health officers are possibly even more important than to younger employees. To make training older employees successful, it is sometimes necessary that the organization first does something about the self-reinforcing prejudices and stereotypes about these employees that undermine their position. Workshops (section 2.11) and training older employees to deal with these issues (section 8.7) can be of help here. In addition, it is often necessary that these older workforce members take more responsibility themselves for their own functioning in the organization again. A training course in self-management (section 8.9) may be useful in this respect.

8.7 Training in personal effectiveness or assertiveness

Training programmes in personal effectiveness, or assertiveness as it is also called, focus on how to deal more effectively with questions and demands from clients, superiors or colleagues. Learning goals may be:

- learning to say no to clients, superiors or colleagues;
- keeping to own priorities and limits;
- counteracting task disturbances;
- learning to explain own dilemmas and impossibilities;
- refusing to act as a serving-hatch;
- dealing with stereotyping and labelling by superiors or colleagues (this issue can also be on the agenda of a workshop with the complete work unit, see section 2.11);
- serving no longer as a scapegoat and learning to deal with harassment by superiors or colleagues;
- dealing better with one's own anger and so keeping contacts and relationships intact by preventing unnecessary conflicts.

Effective techniques here are:

- a good problem analysis, including determining in which situations and with which persons the problems occur in everyday life and keeping a diary of it;
- finding out which ideas and lines of thought underlie this;
- finding out which positive outcomes these problems may have for the individual and which role these play in reinforcing and maintaining this behaviour;
- role playing with video-feedback, in which we also make use of exaggeration and reversal of role behaviour;
- feedback exercises about strong and weak points in this respect.

8.8 Time management

Good time management programs focus on formulating clear and realistic goals and setting priorities (important–unimportant; urgent–not urgent), as well as on phasing, grouping and shielding tasks. We can derive priorities from organizational goals (mission, vision, job demands), personal goals or both. This enables the person to dedicate him- or herself to what really matters, to delegate better and not to spend time on irrelevant activities. This is primarily a matter of becoming aware: what is important and what is not? In addition, trainees learn about causes of unnecessary time loss and may practise all kinds of methods to minimize this time loss. The latter vary from fixed procedures for routine activities and referral, to more rational ways of handling visitors, mail, telephone, e-mail, etc. All this can help to push back all kinds of task disturbances and stress.

As in all forms of training, this is – apart from becoming aware – mainly about practising alternative ways of doing, to develop our own style, which makes us feel alright.

8.9 Self-management and employability

Courses in self-management and employability focus on developing new options for employees of different age groups to become more effective, motivated and creative in their jobs, career and further life. This should lead to more effective steering of one's own life and career.

In such training programmes, it is important that trainees look into what they themselves want and are able to do, as well as what they are allowed and have to do. Which are the basic themes and motives in their life and work? Which are their most important talents? Which chances and limitations do the organization and its environment offer to realize these motives and talents? What in these circumstances would have to change? And how do we go about it? In addition, individuals need to relate these questions to their own life styles. For example, the answers will be different for older and younger employees.

Self-management also extends to life outside of work. So it is important to lead a balanced life, in which there is also room and attention for the following issues.

- Other life realms:
  - family;
  - friends;
  - amusement;
  - public affairs.
- Own health:
  - sufficient sleep and rest;
  - sufficient bodily movement;
  - not too much drinking (alcohol) and smoking;
  - responsible use of medication.
- General knowledge.
- Sense making.

Such a programme has to result in personal goals and a plan that enables the trainees, in interaction with relevant other persons and the organization, to realize these goals for the next years. Group members can also indicate how they can and want to help each other.

8.10 Stress management

Stress management training programs can be aimed at different target groups. These focus on coping with stress and stress prevention. The following outcomes are partially similar to those of training programmes for managers.

- Acquiring a conceptual framework to talk about all this.
- Breaking the taboo on talking about stress at work.
- Actually talking about stress at an earlier stage.
- Being able to notice stress risks and reactions earlier and better.

- Mapping one's own stress sources and reactions, and their underlying causal patterns.
- Some knowledge about interventions.
- Dealing more properly with one's own stress.
- Dealing with crises and traumatic events (hold-ups, accidents, etc.): a so-called 'stress inoculation training course'.

Dependent on the specific course, there are in addition the following outcomes.

- Taking pauses to recuperate, reflect and plan regularly.
- A healthier life style.
- Keeping a stress logbook to get more insight on one's own productivity and stress feelings for a period of one or two weeks.
- Learning to work more sensibly and tracing individual suppositions underlying working insensibly (for example: "I am only a worthwhile person when I do more than the next person").
- Some knowledge about time management and planning.
- Some knowledge about, and skill in, tracing ideas that mean somebody experiences stress earlier (the so-called 'irrational' ideas from the 'Rational-Emotive Therapy' or RET).
- Some skill in preventing harassment and thought stopping.
- Some knowledge of and skill in one or more of the many ways to bring about 'thinking of nothing special', such as breathing techniques, relaxation exercises, guided fantasies, haikido exercises, running, etc.).
- Applications of 'thinking of nothing special', such as:
  - relaxation, refreshing, or centering;
  - asking oneself questions ('focusing');
  - motivating oneself, as well as setting goals for oneself (to work in a more concentrated way or to monitor one's own behaviour).
- Different methods to prepare difficult tasks (behavioural therapeutic methods, such as mental preparation, but also self-suggestion and methods of Gestalt-therapeutic origin, such as 'voice dialogue' and 'internal workshop')

Here too, the important thing is to practise, in order to find an approach that suits you.

8.11 Ergonomic training programmes

Ergonomic training programmes usually are short and consist of some instruction and exercising. We give here the following examples.

- Appropriate working posture and movements (for example: lifting weights properly; proper use of the mouse). The underlying idea is that appropriate postures and movements cause less wear and tear to the body parts in question, as well as less fatigue.
- Dealing properly with dangerous substances.
- Use of protective clothing and safety equipment.

9 INDIVIDUAL COUNSELLING

Individual counselling by an expert professional with a psychotherapeutic background is also an option sometimes, for instance in the case of the following work problems:

- traumatic events at the work site;
- unwanted intimacies;
- serious forms of bullying and of scapegoating;
- burnout.

Counselling can also be applied when the causes of the problems lie outside work, but may still influence the work negatively. Examples are:

- fear of failure;
- type A problems (a rather compulsive work style, characterised by taking on too many tasks, doing several tasks simultaneously, habitual haste, hostility, stereotypical perceptions, thinking in categories of 'black and white' and so on);
- social anxiety and serious submissiveness;
- depression;
- many other serious forms of personal ineffectiveness and psychosocial problems.

Some sessions with a psychotherapist often are useful. Though the techniques used may vary, there is a remarkable preference for all kinds of short variants of cognitive behaviour therapy.

A special form of individual guidance by a corporate welfare worker, nurse or psychologist can take place when an employee returns to his or her work after a lengthy period of illness or work disability. Often, employees have some fear to return, certainly when the work has contributed to the sick leave. The accompanying person sometimes will contact the employee's manager. This is about preparing the return as well as looking whether it is possible to do something about factors that may have contributed to the sick leave.

Lastly, it should be pointed out that personal accompanying, foremost in an informal sense, ideally comes from our own management and colleagues.

10 STRESS CONSULTANTS

When the stress management project has been finished and its results have been anchored in other managerial and policy cycles, the project team members can be (part-time) employed as stress consultants. Individual employees or managers can consult them in the case of stress problems. The stress consultants then may engage in the following actions:

- giving information and advice;
- assessing problems in more detail;
- coaching;
- organizing and conducting a workshop to solve the problem;
- acting as 'confidence persons', for example to employees who feel themselves treated unjustly by a superior, as well as in the case of bullying or unwanted intimacies (in many organizations, this is an official, institutionalized position),
- consulting or bringing in an expert.

References

Arendt, H. (1958) *The Human Condition*. Chicago: University of Chicago Press.

Asch, S.E. (1971) The doctrine of suggestion. In: L.L. Barker and R.J. Kibler (Eds) *Speech Communication Behavior*. Englewood Cliffs, NJ: Prentice Hall.

Bandler, R. and Grinder, J. (1986) *Hypnotherapie*. Haarlem: De Toorts.

Bellow, S. (1982) *The Dean's December*. New York: Pocket Books.

Bernstein, A.J. and Craft Rozen, S. (1989) *Dinosaur Brains*. New York: Ballantine Books.

Breznitz, S. (Ed.) (1983) *The Denial of Stress*. New York: International Universities Press.

Brosschot, J.F. (1991) Stress, perceived control and immune response in man. Dissertation, University of Utrecht.

Cannon, W.B. (1935) Stress and strain of homeostasis. *American Journal of Medical Science*, 1, 1–14.

Covey, S.R. (1989) *The Seven Habits of Highly Effective People*. New York: Simon and Schuster.

Csikszentmihalyi, M. (1990) *Flow: The Psychology of Optimal Experience*. New York: Harper and Row.

Dorpat, T.L. (1985) *Denial and Defense in the Therapeutic Situation*. New York: Aronson.

Eibl-Eibesfeldt, I. von (1970) *Ethology, The Biology of Behavior*. New York: Holt, Rinehart and Winston.

Emlen, J.T. Jr (1958) Defended area? A critique of occasion, territory concept and of conventional thinking. *Ibis*, 99, 352.

Erickson, M.H., Rossi, E.J. and Rossi, S.I. (1976) *Hypnotic Realities*. London: Wiley and Sons.

Gendlin, E.T. (1978) *Focusing*. New York: Everest House.

Goffman, E. (1963) *Behavior in Public Places*. Glencoe, IL: Free Press.

Goffman, E. (1972) *Encounters*. Harmondsworth: Penguin Books.

Gordon, J.R. (1991) *A Diagnostic Approach to Organizational Behavior*. Boston: Allyn and Bacon.

Hall, E.T. (1969) *The Hidden Dimension*. Garden City, NY: Doubleday.

Harré, R. (1979) *Social Being*. Oxford: Blackwell.

Hatfield, E., Cacioppo J.T. and Rapson, R.L. (1994) *Emotional Contagion*. Paris: Cambridge University Press.

Hendricks, G. (1998) *The Ten-second Miracle*. San Francisco: Harper.

Hitchcock, D. and Willard, M. (1995) *Why Teams Can Fail and What to do About it*. Chicago: Irwin Professional Publishing.

Holmes, T.M. and Rahe, R.H. (1967) The social readjustment rating scale. *Journal of Psychosomatic Research*, 11, 213–218.

James, W. (1890/1950) *The Principles of Psychology*. New York: Dover Press.

Kanner, A.D., Coyne, J.C., Schaefer, C. and Lazarus, R.S. (1981) Comparison of two modes of stress management: Daily hassles and uplifts versus major life events. *Journal of Behavioral Medicine*, 4, 1–39.

Karasek, R.A. and Theorell, T. (1990) *Healthy Work. Stress, Productivity and the Reconstruction of Working Life*. New York: Basic Books.

Kaufman, J.H. (1971) Is territoriality definable? In A.H. Esser (Ed.) *Behavior and Environment*. New York: Plenum Press.

Lazarus, R.S. (1966) *Psychological Stress and the Coping Process*. New York: McGraw-Hill.

Lindsey, P.H. and Norman, D.A. (1977). *Human Information Processing*. London/New York: Academic Press.

Meyer, J. (1994) *De psychologie van organisatieverandering* [The Psychology of Organisational Change]. Utrecht: Lemma.

Montaigne, M. de (1580/1981) *Essays*. (14th edn, transl. J.M. Cohen) Harmondsworth: Penguin Books.

Morgan, G. (1986) *Images of Organization*. Beverley Hills/London: Sage Publications.

Noreen, E., Smith, D. and Mackey, J.T. (1995) *The Theory of Constraints and its Implications for Management Accounting*. Montvale, NJ: The North River Press.

Ofman, D.D. (1995) *Bezieling en kwaliteit in organisaties* [Inspiration and Quality in Organizations]. Cothen, Netherlands: Servire.

Razran, G. (1964) The orienting reflex. In: R.C. Harper, C.C. Anderson, C.M. Christensen (Eds) *The Cognitive Processes*. Englewood Cliffs, NJ: Prentice Hall.

Rowell, T. (1972) *Social Behaviour of Monkeys*. Harmondsworth: Penguin Books.

Ryan, K.D. and Oestreich, D.K. (1991) *Driving Fear out of the Workplace*. San Francisco: Jossey-Bass.

Sapolsky, R.M. (1994) *Why Zebras Don't Get Ulcers*. New York and Oxford: Freeman and Company.

Schabracq, M.J. (1987). Betrokkenheid en onderlinge gelijkheid in sociale interacties [Involvement and mutual similarity in social interactions]. Dissertation, University of Amsterdam.

Schabracq, M.J. (1991). *De inrichting van de werkelijkheid* [The Design of Reality]. Amsterdam/Meppel: Boom.

Schabracq, M.J. and Winnubst, J.A.M. (1996a) Mid-career problems. In M.J. Schabracq, J.A.M. Winnubst and C.L. Cooper (Eds) *Handbook of Work and Health Psychology*. Chichester: J. Wiley and Sons.

Schabracq, M.J. and Winnubst, J.A.M. (1996b) Senior employees. In M.J. Schabracq, J.A.M. Winnubst and C.L. Cooper (Eds.) *Handbook of Work and Health Psychology*. Chichester: J. Wiley and Sons.

Schaufeli, W.B. and Buunk, B.P. (1996) Professional burnout. In M.J. Schabracq, J.A.M. Winnubst and C.L. Cooper (Eds) *Handbook of Work and Health Psychology*. Chichester: J. Wiley and Sons.

Schneider, B. (1987) People make the place. *Personnel Psychology*, 40, 437-453.

Selye, H. (1956) *The Stress of Life*. New York: McGraw-Hill.

Semmer, N. (1996) Individual differences, work stress and health. In M.J. Schabracq, J.A.M. Winnubst and C.L. Cooper (Eds) *Handbook of Work and Health Psychology*. Chichester: J. Wiley and Sons.

Senge, P.M., Ross, R., Smith, B., Roberts, C. and Kleiner, A. (1996). *The Fifth Discipline Fieldbook*. London: N. Brealey.

Van de Vliert, E. (1996). Interventions in conflicts. In M.J. Schabracq, J.A.M. Winnubst and C.L. Cooper (Eds.) *Handbook of Work and Health Psychology*. Chichester: J. Wiley and Sons.

von Oech, R. (1998) *A Whack on the Side of the Head: How You Can Be More Creative*. Warner Books.

Willner, P. (1993) Animal models of stress: An overview. In S.C. Stanford and P. Salmon (Ed.) *Stress. From Synapse to Syndrome*. London: Academic Press.

Winnubst, J.A.M., Jong, R.D. de and Schabracq, M.J. (1996). The diagnosis of role strains at work. In M.J. Schabracq, J.A.M. Winnubst and C.L. Cooper (Eds) *Handbook of Work and Health Psychology*. Chichester: J. Wiley and Sons.

Winnubst, J.A.M. and Schabracq, M.J. (1996) Social support, stress and organizations. In M.J. Schabracq, J.A.M. Winnubst and C.L. Cooper (Eds) *Handbook of Work and Health Psychology*. Chichester: J. Wiley and Sons.

Index

accidents 65
adrenaline 42
advising 126–8
age 7, 8, 73
aggression 65
alienation 59
allergy, personal 89
ambiguous tasks 81
anonymity 117–18
appraisal 16
assertiveness training 165–166
attention
    denial 14–16
    discipline of attention as a way
        of coping 12–14
autonomy 154, 155

blind spots 24, 25
brainstorming 121–3
breakdown stage of stress process
    44–5
broadening jobs 153–4
bureaucracy 58–9, 70
burnout 44–5, 75

careers, interventions in 156–60
challenge
    insufficient 83–5
    too much challenge 79–83
civil inattention 12–13
coaching 148–50
cognitive denial 14–16

co-management 161
communication
    about stress management
        project 108–9
    failure of 119, 124, 130, 134–5
    social isolation of senior
        managers and 62
    workshops on 144, 147–8
complaints 126
confidentiality 117–18
conflict 62, 66–67, 82
    workshops on solving conflict
        147–148
control, loss of 38–9
control groups 116
coping
    discipline of attention as a way
        of coping 12–14
    loss of control 38–9
    niches and 22
    organizational culture and 23
    primary and secondary
        appraisal and 16
costs
    financial criteria for goal setting
        115
    hidden costs of stress 6
counselling 169–70
creativity, techniques for boosting
    121–3
culture
    organizational 23–8, 64, 71

research into 110–11
  workshops on calming down
    a 'stress culture' 147

daily hassles 19–20
  systemic factors behind 20–1
deadlines 79–80, 147
decision-making
  resistance by decision-makers
    100–1
  too little decision latitude 84–5
  workshop for project decision-
    makers 97
denial 14–16, 129
  blind spots and 24, 25
difficult tasks 80
discourteous treatment 67–8
distrust, climate of 62
divergent responsibilities 81–2
double task load 76–7

education
  general 164
  see also training
effectiveness training 165–6
effort, stress and 45
emotional contagion 56
employability 7, 67
  training in 166–7
employees
  adjusting workload 151
  career policy 158
  compatibility of valueg and
    goals with organizations
    33–36, 72–76
  confidentiality and anonymity
    117–118
  counselling 169–70
  effective functioning of working
    life 28–38
  employee assistance programs
    (EAPs) 150
  high turnover of 56
  imbalance between work and
    other life realms 76–9
  implementation stage of stress
    management project and 133
  interviews about functioning
    and career 158

involvement in stress
    management project 90
  lay-off 61, 159–60
  negative effects of stress on 4–5
  networking *see* social
    embedding
  outplacement 159–60
  personnel data 117
  poor communication with 62
  promotion 69–71
  replacement 158
  representatives 92, 104
  resistance by 26–8, 73, 101
  secondment 159
  selection policy 157
  working with many different
    people 57
  see also training
employers, responsibilities of 90
engagement, lack of 83–4
enriching jobs 154
environment
  impression of 95
  person–environment (PE) fit 33
  shaping of 11
  turbulent 56
ergonomic training 168–9
ethical systems, safety and 32–3
evaluation
  goal setting 115–16
  stress management project 136–8
everyday life 10–23
experience, concentration of 69
expert presentations 108–9
gggggggggggg
feedback, insufficient 81
fight response 42–3, 50–1
financial criteria for goal setting
    115
flight response 42–3
force field analysis 109–10
freeze response 42–3, 51

general adaptation syndrome
    (GAS) 41
glass ceiling effect 70–1
goals
  compatibility of values and
    goals 70–71

too little compatibility as
source of stress 72–75
too much compatibility as
source of stress 75–6
development in stress
management project 113–19
golden cage syndrome 69

high strain condition 85
human resource management
(HRM) 7, 91, 134, 156–60

illness 5, 53–54, 56, 117
employee assistance programs
(EAPs) 150
implementation stage of stress
management project 131–5
activities 132–3
organizational policy and 134
other stakeholders and 133–4
pitfalls and learning
opportunities 134–5
project team and 133
impossibilities 23, 24
incompatible responsibilities 82
insecurity 65–6
interference 16
daily hassles 19–20
life events 16–18
systemic factors behind 20–21
interventions 139–170
adjusting workload 151
in careers 156–60
coaching 148–50
counselling 169–70
designing 120–124
education and training 160–163
employee assistance programs
(EAPs) 150
job redesign 152–6
stress consultants 170
training 160–169
workshops 97–99, 112, 132,
140–148
interviews about employees'
functioning and career 158
irrelevance, rules of 12

job redesign 152–6
job rotation 159

lay-off 61, 159–60
life events 16–18, 20–21, 76
losing colleagues 61

maintenance stage of stress process
43–4
managers
coaching 148–50
implementation stage of stress
management project and
133–4
insufficient support from 104–5
involvement in stress
management project 90–1
partial reports to 128–30
resistance by 101, 129
social isolation of 62
training for 160–3
workshops for 141–2
matrix organizations 57
mental workload 45, 46
mergers 7, 34, 57, 145
metaphors 122–123
Michigan stress model 33
mistakes 80–81
modelling and emotional
contagion 56
motivation
loss of 52, 112, 124
too great an appeal to personal
motives and talents 81
multinational organizations 57, 59

neatness 29–30
negative hallucinations 15
nervous breakdown 44–5
networks *see* social embedding
newsletters 108
niches 21–2
noncommittal attitude 83–4

occupational health workers 91–92
offices 61, 63–64
open-plan offices 63–4
'one right solution' 105
oracles 123

orderliness 29–30
  as source of stress
    too little orderliness 55–8
    too much emphasis on
      orderliness 58–60
organizational culture *see* culture,
  organizational
orientation response 42–3
outplacement 159–60
overload 40, 41
overtiredness 38
overwork 22

Pareto principle 98
past, workshops on clearing up
  unpleasantness in 146–7
pauses 123
perceptive denial 15
person–environment (PE) fit 33
Peter Principle 69–70
physical barriers to social contact
  61
physicians 91–2
pleasure, loss of 52
positive pressure 5
presentations 108–9
prevention of stress 163–4
privacy, lack of 63–4
productions, workshops on
  optimizing 146
professional training 164–9
progress meetings, presentations
  during 109
project team
  communication and 108–9
  counteracting stress 3–4
  disbanding 134
  implementation stage of stress
    management project and 133
  leader 103
  organizational policy and 134
  training 3, 107–8
  working with projects 102–4
promotion 69–71
psychopaths 66, 157

relationship-building stage of
  stress management plan 90–106
  characteristics 93–5

occasions and causes 90
parties involved 90–2
pitfalls and learning
  opportunities 104–6
political/relational issues
  99–100, 105–6
resistance 100–2
technical and content-oriented
  issues 95–9, 105
working with projects 102–4
reorganizations 57, 61, 145
repetition 10–12, 21
reporting stage of stress
  management plan 124–31
  advising 126–8
  contents of report on stress risks
    127–8
  partial reports to supervisory
    committee and managers
    128–30
  pitfalls and learning
    opportunities 130
  research results 126
research
  into organizational culture
    110–111
  reporting research results 126
resistance
  to change 26–8, 73, 101–2
  in stress management project
    100–2, 129
responsibilities
  divergent 81–2
  incompatible 82
  too little decision latitude 84–5
  unclear 81
roles
  changing perspectives 122
  conflict 82
  double task load 76–7
  role-playing 122, 141
  transitions 60–1

safety 32–3
  as source of stress
    too little safety 65–8
    too much safety 68–71
schizophrenia 59
secondment 159

self-directing teams 155
self-management, training in 166–7
self-pity 45
senior managers 62, 141–142
SMART 115
social contact 22, 154–5
social embedding 30–2
  job redesign for 154–5
  as source of stress
    too little social embedding
      60–3
    too much social embedding
      63–5
  workshops on improving social
    support 147–8
social muzak 30
social skills, training in 162–3
sources of stress 55–86
  challenge
    insufficient challenge 83–5
    too much challenge 79–83
  compatibility of values and
    goals
    too little compatibility 72–5
    too much compatibility as
      source of stress 75–6
  imbalance between work and
    other life realms 76–9
  orderliness
    too little orderliness 55–8
    too much emphasis on
      orderliness 58–60
  safety
    too little safety 65–8
    too much safety 68–71
  social embedding
    too little social embedding
      60–3
    too much social embedding
      63–5
  stress reactions as 54
specialization 69
staff *see* employees
stars 64, 75
stress
  estimation of seriousness of 96
  increased interest in 7–8
  as indicator 1–4, 21

  individual stress reactions 47–54
  nature of 10–46
  negative effects 4–7
  prevention of 163–4
  stages of stress process 39, 41–5
  see also sources of stress; stress
    management
stress consultants 170
stress management
  interventions *see* interventions
  objectives of approach 2–4
  personal position and attitude
    88–9
  plan for 87, 90–138
    step 1: organization and
      consultant form a
      relationship 90–106
    step 2: getting established
      106–13
    step 3: developing specific
      goals 113–19
    step 4: designing
      interventions 120–4
    step 5: reporting 124–31
    step 6: implementation 131–5
    step 7: evaluation 136–8
  time scale 87–8
  training in 167–8
  warning 88
  workshops to create appropriate
    conditions for 142–3
suggestion techniques 123
supervisory committee 104,
  128–130
survivors' syndrome 61, 160
systemic errors, stress as tracer for
  2–4, 21

targets *see* goals
teams
  autonomous task groups and
    self-directing teams 155
  see also project team
technical and professional training
  164–9
technological change 1
tension 51–2
territory 22,.50

tidiness 29–30
time
    time management 166
    time scale of stress management
        plan 87–8
    too few activities to fill time 83
    too little time to do things 79–80
tiredness 38
training
    managers 160–3
    project team 3, 107–8
    in social skills 162–3
    in stress prevention 163–4
    technical and professional 164–9
transitions, role 60–1
traumatic experiences 65
trust 32–33, 61
turnover of employees 56

uncertainty about the future 67
unclear responsibilities 81
underload 40, 41
unspeakables 23, 24, 88, 146–7

unthinkables 23, 24

vague complaints 48
values
    compatibility of values and
        goals 33–6
        too little compatibility as
            source of stress 72–5
        too much compatibility as
            source of stress 75–6
welfare workers 92
wellbeing
    employee assistance programs
        (EAPs) 150
    workshops on optimizing 146
win–win solution 100
work cubicles 61
workers *see* employees
working conditions 37
workload 45–6
    adjusting 151
works councils 92, 104
workshops 97–9, 112, 132, 140–8